designed to last

designed to last

Our Journey of Building an Intentional Home, Growing in Faith, and Finding Joy in the In-Between

TYNDALE
MOMENTUM®

A Tyndale nonfiction imprint

ASHLEY & DINO PETRONE

with SEPTEMBER VAUDREY

Visit Tyndale online at tyndale.com.

Visit Tyndale Momentum online at tyndalemomentum.com.

Visit Ashley Petrone at arrowsandbow.com.

Tyndale, Tyndale's quill logo, *Tyndale Momentum*, and the Tyndale Momentum logo are registered trademarks of Tyndale House Ministries. Tyndale Momentum is a nonfiction imprint of Tyndale House Publishers, Carol Stream, Illinois.

Designed to Last: Our Journey of Building an Intentional Home, Growing in Faith, and Finding Joy in the In-Between

Designed by Julie Chen

For information about special discounts for bulk purchases, please contact Tyndale House Publishers at csresponse@tyndale.com, or call 1-855-277-9400.

Library of Congress Cataloging-in-Publication Data

A catalog record for this book is available from the Library of Congress.

ISBN 978-1-4964-5512-3

Printed in the United States of America

28	27	26	25	24	23	22
7	6	5	4	3	2	1

To my Instagram community,
the kindest, wisest, most talented home-design fanatics I know.
—Ashley

And to Gabe, Gavin, Quinn, and Foxi:
It's an honor to be your parents. We love you so much.
—Ashley and Dino (Mom and Dad)

contents

Part III | Soar

a note from ashley

About five years ago, I had an idea. I pulled Dino aside, looked him in the eye, and said, "Babe, maybe we should write a book."

Dino stared at me in surprise. "Huh? Um, yeah, babe, let's get on that," he said, laughing.

But he saw the earnest look on my face. He knew the joy I got from sharing ideas and inspiration through my blog and Instagram accounts, @arrowsandbow. They provided an artistic outlet for me, a self-employed mom of three little ones. It gave me so much joy to read comments from people who said something I'd posted had empowered them to create a beautiful, welcoming space in their own home. I just love home design, not just because it's creative and fun, but because it brings my people closer. I thought of all the life lessons it had taught me over the past ten years that I'd been married to the man standing before me.

"Okay, let's hear it," he said. And in pure Dino fashion, he dove into the conversation I clearly wanted to have.

"It's like this: I know we don't know everything about life or marriage or whatever." Dino laughed again. "But I keep thinking about my younger self at eighteen or nineteen years old, not married but wanting to be; dating but unhappy; trying to figure out God's place in my life. Then married at twenty after a whirlwind romance and engagement. I wish I'd had someone to shed a little insight into married life, family, and faith—how to build our most important relationships so they endure for the long haul. Someone a few years ahead of me, someone I could relate to."

"Would have helped us both to have that," Dino said.

"We still have so much to learn," I continued, "but we're a few years ahead of some people, and I feel like maybe we have some helpful stuff to share."

"Yeah, maybe," he said. After a brief pause, he nodded. "I think you're right."

Neither of us thought about the book idea again until a year or so ago, when a publisher who followed me on Instagram approached us.

Long story short, we wrote a book.

Although we've only been married for fifteen years, we've crammed some crazy experiences into those years—and plenty of mistakes, too. Man, have we learned a lot! I'm not quite the same stubborn woman who once lived day to day for the next new, shiny thing, hoping it would bring me fulfillment. Slowly, slowly, I'm becoming a more confident, content woman. Dino, too, has matured through these experiences, and we've grown together as a couple.

This book is part memoir, part DIY-design book—an odd combination, I know. The thing is, design is woven into my story so closely that I can't separate the two. I can't fully tell one part of our story without the other.

The first part of each chapter is pure memoir; then you'll find an "At Home with Ashley" section packed with some of my favorite DIY tips and tricks. They're mostly related to home design, but—full confession—I sneaked some relational tips in there too! You've been warned.

I used to think my love for home design was a curse because it so often led to discontentment with what I had—or didn't have. Today I can see how God used my passion for design to enable me not only to improve the homes we've lived in, but also to experience the relationship between intentional design and intentional living. Good design mirrors good living. Read on and see if you agree.

As I mentioned, home design gave me more than just a better-looking house; it introduced me to my incredible community of Instagram friends. If this includes you, thank you! You've watched my design skills grow, given me great ideas, prayed for me, and encouraged my personal growth along the way. I'm forever grateful. You're my favorites! And if you haven't yet checked out our online community at @arrowsandbow, join us! You'll be welcomed aboard wholeheartedly.

> *Good design mirrors good living.*

This book is our story. Dino and I don't know everything. We fail and make mistakes and are far from perfect, as you're about to find out. But we hope that by being open about our lives, sharing the vulnerable parts (gulp!), and simply telling our adventures, you might discover similarities between our journey and yours.

We have a lot in common, you and I. Whether you're married or single, a parent or not, a Christian or an atheist, you're a human like me. You're someone trying to figure out life, make your world better, and become a better person. That's my journey too. Here's what has worked for Dino and me. I hope you find our story helpful as you live out your own.

Ashley Pea

a note from dino

Ash and I wrote this book together, which is how we do life—as true partners. While the two of us hold many of the same values, our perspectives are almost always different (ahem—opposite!). So rather than trying to write as one voice, we each wrote our own sections in each chapter, with Ash telling the main story and DIY-design stuff while I provide parts of my own story and add some color commentary. You'll notice the Dino text has a different font and style (like what you're seeing right now) to make the transitions between our segments clear. (The other clue would be the letter *D* that begins each of my parts.)

The writing process turned out to be a smooth, awesome ride, and we hope you enjoy the read.

PART I

spark

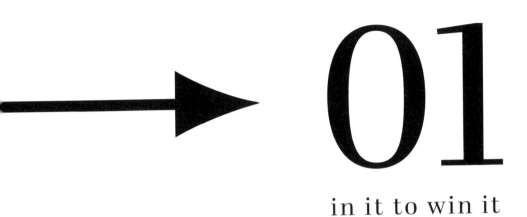

01

in it to win it

"So you wanna?" Dino asked, pulling a small velvet box from the pocket of his shorts. He opened it to face me. Inside was a stunning engagement ring.

I stood there in the beach parking lot, shocked—staring first at the ring and then at the man I'd been dating for all of three whole weeks.

Three weeks! What?

Let me back up.

Dino and I had known each other since we were kids. He'd played on a soccer team with my older brother, Ryan, in our small town of Lynden, Washington. Our parents had become friends and kept in touch even after my family moved to

California and his to Las Vegas. But until a few weeks before, I'd not seen Dino since I was in eighth grade and he was a senior in high school.

Then along came our moms, who just so happened to be close friends.

D When my mom told me that Lori Fabian and her daughter, Ashley, were coming to visit her and my dad in Las Vegas for the weekend and suggested I come home for a visit, too, I didn't give it much thought. I recalled Ashley only as Ryan's kid sister, a blonde wisp of a girl, cheering for her brother from the sidelines of our high school soccer games. Now I was twenty-four and single, having broken up with a longtime girlfriend six months prior. I'd just run a marathon and was focusing on my health, figuring out who I was without said girlfriend, and having fun with my roommates at Cal State Long Beach. I was in no hurry to start dating again. *But sure, Mom, I'll be glad to make the five-hour drive home to Vegas to visit you and Dad for the weekend—and say hi to your friend and her kid.* And so I did.

Then the doorbell rang, and I opened my parents' door.

There stood Ashley, blonde and beautiful with a dazzling smile. *Heyo! Total babe.* I couldn't believe this was the same little kid from my soccer team days. She had just turned twenty, and she took my breath away.

Our moms knew exactly what they were doing. This trip had been their idea, after all. For the past three years, I'd been stuck in a destructive relationship with my boyfriend back home. He didn't treat me well and had cheated on me more than once. I wasn't happy, but I wasn't sure how to break it off.

Too often, I'd been trying to find my value through unhealthy relationships. I'd grown up in a Christian home, but for me that had been more about a list of rules than a relationship with God. And at the fresh age of twenty, I was still trying to figure out who I was.

My mom had been worried about me, and Dino's mom wanted him to find a nice girl, so here I was in Vegas. I walked up to the house, and Mom nudged me forward to ring the doorbell. The door opened.

"Hey!" Dino said, smiling. "C'mon in!"

There stood a tall, dark, and handsome man—with no shirt on, mind you. Had he just gone for a run? I was speechless. *Boyfriend back home? What boyfriend?*

Dino invited us in and led us toward the back patio, and when we stepped outside, the wind off the desert was gusting like crazy. My hair went everywhere.

"'The wind was angry that day, my friend,'" he said, a slight tweak on a famous one-liner from *Seinfeld*'s George Costanza.

This guy knows Seinfeld! *I like him already.*

From the moment I walked into the house that day in Vegas, everything seemed effortless with Dino. We just clicked. He seemed genuinely interested in everything I had to say. As we got to know each other a bit during those first few hours, I felt so at ease, as if we'd never lost touch since those soccer-game days. He was kind, funny, and supportive as I talked, which gave me all the confidence in the world. Unlike past relationships where I felt I had to perform, I quickly realized that with Dino, I could simply be Ashley.

I'm pretty sure the parents noticed how well their matchmaking plan was working because a couple of hours later, they had to make an "emergency" trip to the grocery store, leaving Dino and me alone in the backyard. So subtle.

We got lost in silly conversations about our favorite TV shows and challenged each other to see who knew the most one-liners from *Seinfeld*. I should have taken our mutual love of that show as the first sign that Dino was the one for me.

Dino knew I had a boyfriend, and as the day progressed, I could tell he was doing his best to hold back with me. *Solid guy right there.*

As I looked across the table at Dino over dinner, I had a major light-bulb moment—one that had taken me reconnecting with a guy I hadn't seen since I was thirteen to understand: *There's more out there than the type of guy I've been dating—and maybe I deserve more.*

Growing up, my parents had insisted I go to youth group at our church. I figured I was expected to date squeaky-clean guys like them. But I never did. I chose jerks every time. I didn't realize there were decent, down-to-earth guys who were actually cute (or hotties with a body like Dino's) and who weren't dorks but had a solid faith. Sitting at that table, I realized I was stuck in a relationship back home that was very unhealthy. I was settling.

In just one afternoon with Dino, it hit me: *I don't want to live the rest of my life settling.* Even if nothing were to become of my natural chemistry with this guy, I knew I could do better than my current relationship. I must do better. I deserved better.

The two moms and I had headed downtown to do some shopping. As we drove, I knew I needed to end things with my boyfriend back home. So what did I do? What any normal girl would do: I broke up with him over the phone from the back seat of my mom's car in the parking lot of a T.J. Maxx.

As they parked the car and got out, I hesitated. "I'll be right in, guys!" I said. "Just give me a sec. No biggie—just gonna break up with my boyfriend of three years over the phone. Grab a basket for me!"

The moms exchanged a sly look and then smiled.

"No problem, honey!" my mom said. "Take *allll* the time you need!"

Breaking up with someone over the phone sounds harsh, but it wasn't as bad as it sounds. That boyfriend and I were both unhappy in the relationship, and we'd been talking about breaking up for weeks. My call came as no surprise, and the entire con-

versation took less than three minutes. We both knew it was over. *Done.*

As I hung up the phone, a deep peace settled over me. I felt liberated. I headed into the T.J. Maxx, and after a good thirty-second cry in the purse department, I was ready to move on with my life. Also, snatching up a few great deal-finds definitely helped. I mean, it would have been a shame not to bond with the two hopeful moms over some shopping!

The moms and I paid for our treasures and headed to Starbucks to meet Dino and his dad, Dean, for coffee. The news that I was now unattached and available made its way back to Dino in record time. (Thanks, parents!) As soon as we sat down, it was clear that the connection between Dino and me had ramped up a notch. Now that I was a free woman, Dino was a little flirtier and I was digging it.

The rest of that Saturday was a blast. Dino and I spent every moment together, and it gave us a good chance to get to know each other beyond the obvious mutual attraction.

As our little weekend getaway neared its end, our moms began scheming again. Dino had a test to take back at college on Monday morning and was planning to head home Sunday night.

"One more day, Dino!" my mom begged over dessert that night. "Can't you just stay for one more day? You can do a makeup test!"

She was such a bad influence, but Dino played along.

"Lori," he said, pointing to her dessert, "if you eat that entire brownie and ice cream in two minutes, I'll stay."

My mom was never one to turn down a challenge. She stared down at the brownie in front of her, then picked up her fork. "Deal!" she said and dove in.

"Okay, okay!" Dino said, stopping her after a few bites. "Don't make yourself sick! I'll stay."

That extra night together really solidified the start of our relationship. We went on a date to the movies and let the sparks fly. Dino tried super hard to take it slow since I was coming out of a three-year relationship. We didn't even hold hands. But it was clear to both of us that this relationship was going somewhere.

D The next day, Lori and Ashley headed back home to Camarillo, California, and I headed to Cal State Long Beach to take my makeup test. Before we left, Lori and I decided to caravan since we'd be driving along the same stretch of Interstate 15 for the first few hours. Ash hopped in my car for the first leg of the trip.

We stopped at our agreed-upon halfway point to get gas and swap passengers. While Ash was in the restroom, Lori began filling up her car. I walked over to her, a little nervous.

"Hey," I said, shoving my hands deep in my pockets and giving her a sideways grin, "I *really* like your daughter."

"Um, I know," Lori said, smiling back. "It's a little obvious. Seems your feelings are mutual."

Yesss!

Over the next three weeks Dino and I relied on instant messaging to stay in constant contact. Remember IM? This was before texting, and neither of us were big phone talkers, so IM was our go-to thing.

I worked as a stylist's assistant at a hair salon in Westlake Village, about sixty-five miles west of Dino's apartment in Costa Mesa, with Los Angeles in between. A couple of days after I returned home from Vegas, my stylist went out of town so I had some time off. I headed to Costa Mesa to visit Dino.

He shared a two-bedroom apartment with three roommates. Let's just say it was definitely a college guys' apartment. The furniture was mismatched and sparse, clearly bought at garage sales or found on the curb. Strange smells lingered in the air, and the sofa and carpet boasted twin stains that looked like someone had spilled Froot Loops and forgotten to clean it up. That disgusting sofa was my bed during my stay, so I took it upon myself to grab one of Dino's clean sweatshirts and cover the couch pillows with it while I slept!

Ash agreed to come down for a couple of days to visit. At first, I was thrilled she'd said yes. Then I began to panic. What was I going to do with her? I had no idea.

Let's be honest: Ash was way out of my league—a fact my roommates had reminded me of far too often ever since I'd told them about her and shown them pictures.

I felt suddenly insecure. *What can I do to impress this woman?* Certainly, this apartment wouldn't do it. Then it hit me: *I'll take her for a ride on my motorcycle!* In my nervousness, I went for the most "show-off" activity I could think of. What woman can resist a guy on a motorcycle, right?

When Ash arrived, she took my breath away once again. Even though we'd talked and had been instant messaging constantly since Vegas, this was only the second time we'd seen each other in person. I was reminded just how remarkable and beautiful she was.

I gave her a quick tour of the apartment before hitting her up: "Want to head to the beach on my motorcycle? No plans. We can just see where the day takes us."

"Sounds great!" she said.

We loaded the bike with towels and a picnic, and I fired it up. Ash hopped on back and put her hands around my waist. It felt electric. Her touch was so natural, so confident. She wasn't fearful of holding me tight or in any way uncomfortable with me. All my insecurities instantly melted away. There was something about her touch that instantly gave me confidence in myself. This woman made me feel like I could take on the world. Everything about being with her felt so natural, so normal, so right.

We took off, the breeze in our hair and sun on our faces.

And a mile later, my bike broke down.

If you're unfamiliar with motorcycles, here's what you need to know: They're surprisingly heavy and hard to move when they're not in drive. As my bike puttered to a stop, Ash jumped off and quickly got behind me, pushing and helping maneuver the bike out of traffic. *This woman is no mere princess,* I thought. *She's tough!*

Without speaking a word, we both instinctively clicked into partner mode, each doing what was needed in the moment to get the bike and ourselves to safety.

Ashley's reaction shocked me. Why was I so struck by her hopping off the bike and helping? Then I remembered: A few weeks earlier I had been on a date with a girl who was more of a friend than anything else, but while driving her home, my Jeep broke down. (Clearly, vehicle maintenance wasn't high on my priority list—or within my budget—in those college days!)

I got out of the Jeep and began pushing it to the side of the road. This girl didn't budge; she just sat there in the car. Not only was she apparently unwilling to help me, but she made things harder by adding her weight to the car for a Dino-powered ride.

Ashley's reaction was such a stark contrast. Without me asking, she did what was needed, adding her physical strength to help solve the problem. In those few moments, I learned a ton about who she was—and what kind of partner she'd someday be.

It didn't stop there. During every minute I spent with her in the coming weeks, whether in person, IM'ing, or on the phone, I felt like we were talking soul to soul. We finished each other's sentences, shared so many of the same values, and had so much in common when it came to what we wanted in life. We could talk for hours.

We even laughed at the same odd things. Once when my roommate Greg dropped something on his toe and yelped in pain, we both burst out laughing. *Same weird sense of humor? Check.* Everything just clicked.

After the motorcycle breakdown and those first couple of days together, I was beyond sold on wanting a lifetime of days with this woman. Not to sound overly dramatic, but it felt as if I had been living in a world of black-and-white my whole life, and now I was seeing in color for the first time. I couldn't stand the idea of going back to monochromatic living. I wanted to be around Ash all the time. She told me she felt the same.

From that weekend on, we spent every possible waking second together.

When I wasn't at Dino's apartment, we spent our time IM'ing. We even watched *Seinfeld* reruns and other favorite shows together while chatting via IM or the phone.

By this point in our lives, we both knew what we wanted in a life partner. Each of us had been in several serious long-term relationships, and although we were only twenty-four and twenty years old and had been dating for only three weeks, I knew Dino was someone I could build a life with, and that's exactly what I wanted to do.

We began talking about marriage early and often. After just a few weeks, we felt so connected, and it wasn't a mere physical connection. In fact, we'd shown great restraint physically. The chemistry was certainly there, but it was much more than that. It was a connection of our souls.

D In the few weeks since Vegas, we had been together every day but two. From the day we met, I had known this woman was a perfect fit for me. But wasn't it too soon to get engaged? I believe marriage is for a lifetime, and I knew if I were to marry Ashley, it would be a forever commitment. I didn't want to make a mistake and marry her on impulse.

At twenty-four, I was young, but I was wise enough to know that when it came to making a huge decision like this, I needed the input of others who knew me and knew Ash. I needed confirmation from people I respected. Was I just infatuated with this amazing woman? Or could others see what I saw in us—this perfect fit, this effortless synergy?

First, I talked to my roommates. "What's your take on things with me and Ash?" I asked. "I'm serious about spending the rest of my life with this woman, and I want to ask her to marry me. I trust you guys and your judgment. Are you seeing things like I'm seeing them?"

The three of them had spent almost as much time with Ash at our apartment as I had. They'd also hung out with her on their own when I'd been in class or at work. They'd seen firsthand how we clicked. One by one, they looked me in the eye and basically said, "You'd be a fool not to marry this woman."

Their input gave me confidence that I wasn't crazy. Ash and I truly did have something special.

I then spoke to my parents, Ash's mom, and her closest friends. I wanted their input and their blessing in asking her to marry me. They all affirmed what I sensed in our relationship: This was right. They all told me to go for it. But the biggest conversation was yet to come: I called Ash's dad, Glen, and asked him to meet me at Starbucks the following day.

I'm a traditional guy, and it was important to me that I honor Glen's role in Ash's life. It's not like he made me feel I needed his permission to marry Ash. She was an adult who could decide her own future, after all. But I definitely wanted his blessing. If he didn't feel good about me marrying his daughter,

After just a few weeks, we felt so connected. The chemistry was certainly there, but it was much more than that. It was a connection of our souls.

I legit didn't want to go through with it until he did. I knew the parents were happy that we were together. Still, the short time we'd been dating was sure to raise Glen's eyebrows, and I was a little nervous.

Before meeting with her dad the next day, I drove to Ash's apartment as a surprise. We didn't have plans, but she had the afternoon off, so we just hung out. Once again, I was reminded just how effortless it was to be with this woman. We didn't need plans or entertainment. We clicked so well, just being together.

Ash had no idea I'd spent the last few days talking with friends and family about marrying her—or that I was meeting with her dad that evening. When it was time for my secret meeting with Glen, I made up an excuse about having to run a work errand nearby. "I love you, Ash," I said, hugging her as I left. It was the first time I'd said those words out loud.

"I love you too, babe," she said.

When Glen sat down at my Starbucks table, I realized I didn't really have a planned speech, so I just told him what was on my heart.

"Your daughter is amazing," I said. "More than that, it just feels so natural to be with her. I realize it's only been a few weeks since we've been dating—"

"Two weeks, to be exact," Glen interjected.

"Yes, only two weeks," I continued, "but here's the thing: I want to ask your daughter to marry me. We've spent almost every day together since Las Vegas, and we've spent hours and hours talking—about everything. We want the same things in life. Our families share the same values. And I want to spend the rest of my life with your daughter."

Glen wasn't surprised. I'm sure Lori or my mom had leaked to him why I wanted to have coffee. And he came prepared with questions: "How are you going to provide financially? Can you support yourself and a family? Where will you live? What's your plan for marrying Ashley?"

I had solid answers. I was about to graduate from college and had a good job. I was making a decent living. Ash was supporting herself, too, in an apartment where we could live after we got married. I wanted to be an honorable man by her, and we would wait till we got married to have sex.

"That's all good," Glen said, "but Dino, what I really want to know is this: Do you love my daughter? Have you told her you love her? Has she said she loves you?"

"Yes, sir," I said, grateful for my earlier conversation with Ash. "I absolutely love your daughter, and she tells me she loves me, too."

"All right, then," he said. "Yes. Yes, you have my blessing to marry my daughter."

And now to that beach parking lot and the velvet box . . .

Dino's "So you wanna?" was not perhaps the most romantic or conventional marriage proposal in the world. But let's face it: Nothing about our relationship had been conventional. Romantic, yep! Conventional? No.

Without hesitation, I said yes.

We set our wedding date for September 24. Yeah, a four-month engagement fits with our form of crazy.

the two become one

We chose not to live together before our wedding because we wanted to save sex for our wedding night. But I'm not gonna lie—there were some hot make-out seshes in there!

I remember our first kiss so well. After the failed motorcycle picnic on the first day I visited Dino, we decided to walk to an outdoor mall in Newport Beach, not far from his apartment. He hadn't even held my hand yet! Inside I was like, *Come on, buddy, you're killin' me! Make a move!*

As we walked toward the Cheesecake Factory where we had dinner reservations, my patience hit a wall. I took the initiative and grabbed his hand.

"Whoa, whoa, whoa! You can't make the first move!" he said.

Apparently, I'd bruised his Italian ego and stolen his thunder.

"Oh, yeah?" I replied, grinning. "What are you going to do about it?"

He turned me around and pulled me in close for our first kiss.

It was worth the wait.

The handholding/first kiss scenario is a good snapshot of our personalities. We're both pretty strong and domineering. My role model of how to be a woman was my mother. We are very close, and she's a strong, confident woman. She taught me, "If you want something done, you do it yourself." And there is no such thing as "No." You find a way.

Dino, on the other hand, had a stereotypical Italian father as his dominant role model. His dad is a hardworking, godly man with a commanding personality. We both carried a bit of unhealthy bossy-pants baggage into our relationship.

About two months before our wedding, we got into one of those wonderful tangles that people inevitably have when they're first getting to know each other. Neither of us can remember how the argument started, but it definitely had a whole bunch of this in the middle:

Dino: Well, you have to do what I say because I'm the boss!

Me: What? Um, heck no! *No way* are you the boss of me! I'm my own woman, and you can't tell me what to do!

Can you hear both of our parents in these words? The fight ended with us hanging up the phone on each other. I then cried for a few hours, basically assuming our wedding was off. There was no way I was going to marry a guy who acted like this. And I'm sure I wasn't looking so appealing to him anymore either.

 Hanging up the phone after that fight just about tore my heart out. I didn't even know what we were fighting over, and I couldn't stand the idea of not resolving this. I needed to make things right with Ash and knew I couldn't just carry on as normal while the most amazing person in my life was upset with me. I had no doubt we would figure it out.

I needed to see Ashley in person; to look her in the eye and apologize; to resolve our disagreement; to be with her and feel her touch; to make sure she understood that with all my heart, I just wanted what was best for her and, ultimately, what was best for us. I prayed she wasn't so upset with me that this was unsolvable.

This was the beautiful beginning of us breaking away from our former selves and beginning a journey of "two becoming one."

It was six o'clock in the evening, and I was in Costa Mesa. She was ninety miles away in Camarillo, and I'd have to drive through the heart of Los Angeles traffic if I wanted to see her that night. I got in my car and floored it, pushing the speed limit for the next three hours as I drove to her apartment.

At around nine o'clock, I heard a knock on my door. I opened it, and there stood Dino—the man I'd fallen in love with just a few short months ago. He had driven through Friday night rush-hour traffic to come and make things right between us.

Dino didn't say a word. He just reached out to me and wrapped me in his arms. Holding tightly to each other, we started crying and apologizing.

I was such a stubborn mule back then. I truly believe that if Dino hadn't humbled himself and initiated reconciliation that night, I never would have. And perhaps we wouldn't be married today.

This was the beautiful beginning of us breaking away from our former selves and beginning a journey of "two becoming one."

And a few months later we were married.

designing on a budget

Our first home together was an overpriced apartment in Camarillo, the town where I'd grown up. As a new bride, I was super excited to decorate our place.

From an early age, I had always been fascinated with the quick transformation I could give my bedroom simply by moving the furniture around. Mom used to tease me about how often I rearranged my room, but the new look made all the difference to me, not just aesthetically, but for my mood. It was like a fresh start every time.

I even liked helping my friends rearrange their rooms. Once when I was in eighth grade, I spent the night at my best friend's house. Let's just say she wasn't the tidiest girl. So the next morning while she was in the shower, I raced around her room cleaning, organizing, and rearranging. It was a race against the clock!

When she stepped into her room half an hour later while towel drying her hair, she stopped in her tracks. I'll never forget the look of delight on her face. By simply getting rid of clutter, organizing what was left, and moving some furniture, I was

QUICK TIPS

▶ Buy quality furniture secondhand.
▶ Use mood lighting to create ambience.

▶ Create free space by avoiding the temptation to cram too much in a room.
▶ Paint one wall to give a room a whole new look.

able to show her the room's potential. With a little rearranging, her space felt more open and better reflected her personality.

Kind of a weird story, but as you can see, the desire to bring beauty, peace, and personality to physical spaces has always been in me.

Fast-forward to my first apartment as a newly married woman, and those habits stuck with me! The apartment was tiny and pretty standard as apartments go—white walls, beige carpets, cheap countertops, and window blinds. Our budget was tiny, too, but I still had big ideas for our first home together. So what's a girl to do? I got creative on how to make that small space pop.

I loved scavenging garage sales to find unique pieces, stuff I knew we could never afford at a furniture store but that would make a fun statement in our little home. We left Dino's Froot Loops–stained couch behind with his roommates and found a leather love seat, recliner, and cool lamp that made it look like actual grown-ups lived there—all for $125. I kept stopping by T.J. Maxx till I found the perfect throw pillows, candles, and area rug that pulled it all together. I was so proud.

It doesn't take a huge budget to create a space you'll love. It's all about creating ambience and making tiny changes that reflect your personality.

DESIGNING ON A BUDGET

Don't let the size of your wallet keep you from creating a beautiful environment. Here are four simple, affordable ways you can transform your home on a budget:

>>> **Buy secondhand.** If your budget cannot support a room full of expensive new furniture, then garage sales, estate sales, flea markets, rummage sales, and apps like Craigslist, Facebook Marketplace, and OfferUp will be your new best friends. So many of my favorite pieces today—both furniture and decor items—are quality pieces I purchased secondhand. It feels great to discover and restore a piece that is old and one-of-a-kind, or even to purchase something brand-new at a majorly discounted price. It's like a treasure hunt!

>>> **Use mood lighting.** Candles and a string of twinkle lights are inexpensive ways to create ambience in any space. I'm pretty sure this was one thing that drew Dino in while we were dating. I lit pillar candles on practically every tabletop in the apartment and thumb-tacked strings of twinkle lights across the living-room ceiling. He loved how cozy the mood lighting made my apartment feel. It wasn't all bright with fluorescent ceiling lights or floor lamps blazing at full blast. There's just something about mood lighting that draws people into a home and makes them want to stay.

>>> **Don't overfill.** Packing your home with too much furniture, decor pieces, or wall hangings overstimulates the senses and creates stress. In my first apartment, I discovered that the more I filled it, the more I wanted to clean it out. Give yourself and your guests room to breathe, especially in a small apartment or house. With minimal furnishings, you create free space. You can see what you have, love what you own, and feel at peace in your clutter-free zone.

>>> **Paint one wall.** As a young girl who constantly rearranged her room, I developed a love for the transforming power of paint. If you can paint your space—even just one contrast wall—go for it. It can truly change a room's whole vibe. Be bold and have fun! If you don't like the result, just paint over it!

02

ten and
a half months
of crying

If you're brave enough to say goodbye, life will reward you with a new hello.

— PAULO COELHO, *The Alchemist*

After our honeymoon, I put my cosmetology license to good use and began working at a nearby hair salon. Dino had a job as a website developer for a large church. He wasn't trained in software development—he had just graduated as a finance major at Cal State Long Beach—but he'd obviously needed a job during college—you know, to pay for all his broken-down Jeeps and busted motorcycles . . .

Did I mention that Dino had no training in coding? (Coding

is geek speak for writing the back-end instructions that tell a website how to function.) His boss simply knew he was the sort of guy who could figure things out, so they threw a book on his desk and said, "Here you go! You have four months to learn how to code."

Dino is probably the most hardworking person I know. He loves a good challenge, and this was one he was more than willing to take on. He soon developed a love for all things coding, and that was the beginning of his career in the technology world.

what happens in vegas

Five months into our newlywed year, we got a call from Dino's parents in Las Vegas. "Kids, we're moving to Northern California in a month," they announced. "How would you feel about renting our home here in Vegas?" They threw out a ridiculously affordable price.

Their beautiful three-thousand-square-foot, four-bedroom home with a yard? For less than we're currently paying for an overpriced one-bedroom apartment—with upstairs neighbors whose, um, nightly bedroom antics are nothing if not loud and enthusiastic?

Hmm . . . Let's think about it . . .

"We're in!" we said without hesitation.

Dino's boss gave him a thumbs-up to work remotely, and I put in my two-week notice at the salon. After packing up our little place, we drove north. My dad had commitments at work he couldn't break, but my mom was free and willing to help with the trip, so she followed behind our U-Haul in her cute little sports car. It was a sweet retracing of our earlier trip along Interstate 15, caravanning home from Vegas after the weekend when Dino and I had first reconnected.

For someone like me who loves rearranging a room, the first days in a new home are so much fun. I mean, everything is so new! We were moving into a huge, gorgeous, fully furnished house. What's not to love?

Once we arrived in Vegas, Dino was pretty preoccupied getting his home office set up and getting back to work. This left my mom and me plenty of time to unpack.

My mom is my partner in crime when it comes to having an eye for design in a new space. As we walked from room to room, we brainstormed the kind of small changes we could make to a beautiful house that didn't actually belong to Dino and me.

"What if we head out tomorrow and search for some baskets at a thrift store," she said. "They would cozy up the kitchen if you placed them on those upper shelves above the cabinets."

In my mind's eye, I pictured Dino and me living in Vegas happily ever after, probably forever. We had cheap rent, a giant house, and a job Dino loved. What could possibly go wrong?

But as my mom's visit was winding down, I started to feel a twinge of sadness. Dino and I were young, and I was moving far from my parents for the first time. My mom and I enjoyed a super tight relationship, and I'd never lived more than twenty minutes away. I was starting to miss her already, and she hadn't even left yet.

When it was time for Mom to head home, Dino and I walked her to her car. My family has this tradition for saying goodbye. When one of us leaves, both the person staying and the one driving off wave goodbye for as long as possible, until they're out of sight. It's so dramatic, but it's so us that I love it.

As my mom pulled out of the driveway, Dino and I stood waving goodbye for an excessive amount of time, and my eyes filled with tears. I realized that for the first time ever, I would be four hours from my parents. I had no friends nearby and no job. I felt all alone in Las Vegas. And thus began my ten and a half months of crying.

Looking back, I can see how little I knew about real hardships. Those lessons were yet to come. But at this point in my young life, I was heartbroken. I mean, there were a few happy tears too. I was excited. I was a new bride with an amazing husband in this big house in a new city. There was so much to explore! So much to do together! And because we didn't really know anyone else in town, I thought the move could be a great way for us to grow closer as a couple.

But as days became weeks and weeks became months, it seemed like often—too often for my liking—Dino didn't want to do anything fun in his free time. He didn't want to go out and explore. Most days, he was content just staying home, sitting on the sofa, and playing his Xbox.

video games?

During our quickie engagement, Dino had not once mentioned that he liked to play video games. I mean, with all those long convos we had, all that IM'ing, and all the deep soul connecting we did, you'd think that maybe a hard-core personal interest would pop up as a topic of discussion, right?

Nope.

So about three months into wedded bliss, here's how I found out about Dino's passion for gaming:

Dino: Hey, babe, Caleb wants to do an all-nighter tonight. That cool with you?

Me: Um, who? And what did you say? An all-nighter? *What does that even mean? A slumber party for boys?*

Dino: Yeah, we're gonna stay up all night and play video games together online.

Me: Oh! You like video games? *Who knew?*

Imagine my Scooby-Doo-like reaction. *Ruh-roh!* I, of course, being the new girl in Dino's world, wanted to be the super cool wife, so I obliged. I went to bed alone while he stayed up all night on the sofa, playing video games online with his buddy. What I didn't realize then was that this was what most of our fights would be about for the next few years.

Within a few months of moving to Vegas, Dino had been offered a great new job at a local tech company. He gave his two-week notice at the remote church job in Southern California and began a new challenge. I got a job at a hair salon down the street.

Vegas had been on an upward-growth curve for many years, but around the time we moved in, the housing market began to crash as the Great Recession hit. People were losing their jobs, and everyone was moving. On our street alone, neighbors all around us lost their homes to foreclosure. Our once-cozy neighborhood now felt eerie. It was like living in a ghost town. This made it really hard to make new friends.

It didn't help that Dino and I had begun living parallel lives. He'd go to work, come home, and start playing video games. I'd go to work, then on my way home I'd go shopping, trying to fill a void of loneliness with material things. I'd spend the rest of my evening crying, feeling sorry for myself and resenting Dino for sitting on the sofa playing video games. So healthy!

My natural love for design and finding deals was becoming my "drug of choice" to solve my lack of contentment and my loneliness. Whenever I watched a TV show featuring a new decor style or visited someone's house with a look different from mine, I would immediately get this bug to switch out all my decor accessories to fit that new style. Farmhouse? *Cool!* Boho? *I'm in!* Industrial steampunk? *Done!*

One day after work, I got an urge to give our family room a shabby chic vibe. I could see the whole thing in my mind's eye. I spent the entire next Saturday shopping and having so much fun letting my imagination run wild. I justified my purchases because I was being thrifty and really only picking up little items like blankets, pillows, art, rugs, and other basic decor. When I got home, Dino was in his office gaming. I quickly removed all the more formal-looking stuff in the family room and swapped it for my new purchases. *Wow! What a difference!* The room looked really great, and I felt a little less lonely.

Then the guilt set in. That room had been perfectly fine as is. It didn't need a remodel, and I didn't need to spend that money. Dino had repeatedly asked me to stick to our agreed-upon budget.

By the time Dino came out from his office, I was in full-fledged defense mode. "Babe, what did you do?!" Dino asked when he stepped into the family room.

"I only spent like $65!" I said. "Don't you love how great it looks?"

And there went our evening. We got into yet another fight about the money I'd spent. Dino felt his budget concerns had gone unheard, and I ended up crying. Lather, rinse, repeat.

I would love to say I cried because of our arguments, but the truth was I just wasn't happy inside. I didn't know who I was. I was searching for answers in deals and decor. It was like my wallet and my heart were in a constant battle. I knew shopping wasn't going to solve my problem, but I couldn't stop, no matter how much Dino and I argued about it. I'd been judging Dino for his obsessive video-game habit—yet here I was with an obsession of my own.

Although I felt God had given me an eye for design, I was using that talent in all the wrong ways. I was blatantly ignoring my husband's concerns, blasting through our very modest income, and trying to fill the emotional, relational, and spiritual gaps in my life with material things. It wasn't working.

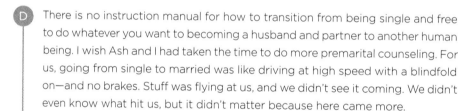

There is no instruction manual for how to transition from being single and free to do whatever you want to becoming a husband and partner to another human being. I wish Ash and I had taken the time to do more premarital counseling. For us, going from single to married was like driving at high speed with a blindfold on—and no brakes. Stuff was flying at us, and we didn't see it coming. We didn't even know what hit us, but it didn't matter because here came more.

I now see all of the faults in my behavior, in my priorities, and in how much time I was wasting playing video games. I was being the opposite of the kind of husband I wanted to be.

Ashley's whole family was really close. Even now that she and her brother were grown, she talked with her parents all the time, and they saw each other often. For her twenty-first birthday, her whole family came to celebrate. Ash's face just radiated that night, and I knew she knew she was loved beyond measure.

I envied how close her family was—and how much she loved them. I wanted to develop that same kind of core family unit with my wife. But I didn't want to bother doing the work to earn that type of relationship. I didn't want to change my habits, give my wife more attention, or partner together to grow our relationship. I was ill-equipped to work on my marriage.

To make matters worse, when things weren't going well for Ash, I would disengage instead of leaning in and trying to help her solve the problem. My obsession with video games began long before I started dating Ash. For me, it wasn't about escaping reality into a make-believe world; rather, it was about completing a puzzle. It fit how my brain is wired to solve problems. I loved trying to figure out strategy and putting pieces together. I could turn on my Xbox and give my brain a little workout that was different from any challenge I faced in real life. It was mental exercise, which for me was fun.

But now that Ash and I were struggling, it became clear that I was choosing to exercise my brain with video games rather than seeking to meet her needs, which weren't even on my radar. If she had an issue with something, I figured that was her responsibility, not mine. I just wanted to fulfill my own needs and not worry about hers.

I write software code for a living, which also fits how my brain works. In coding, when you find a solution, that's it. Done. One plus one always equals two. Marriage is not like that. Marriage is more art than technology. I couldn't code our relationship into working. I couldn't find any variable that would quickly and easily solve what was going on, so instead of seeing our struggles as a personal growth opportunity, I chose a strategy of avoidance. I dove deeper into work and video games.

Bad idea. Marriage is not two people living in one household; it's two people becoming one entity, unique but united. If one of us has a problem, we both have a problem. For the first twenty-four years of my life, if I was hungry, I would eat. If I was tired, I'd go to bed. If I wanted something, I'd go get it. Me, me, me. Then all of a sudden when I said, "I do," everything changed. Another person's needs, wants, and feelings demanded my attention. I didn't understand, nor did I want to.

Of course, in marrying Ashley, I also got all the benefits of having this amazing woman as my partner in life. But I wanted only the good parts, not the ones that were hard, that required sacrifice on my part. *You're sad?* I would think. *Then go fix it. I'll work on my stuff, you work on yours, and we'll meet in the middle.*

Ash and I were now married, and for us, this meant that we were

> *Marriage is not two people living in one household; it's two people becoming one entity, unique but united.*

now one. In neglecting my wife, I was neglecting a part of myself. By focusing only on Dino, I was actually hurting the other half of me.

Don't get me wrong—Ash and I loved each other deeply. But during those early years of our marriage when we were trying to figure out how to make our marriage work, I made little effort to connect with her. Playing video games helped me relax and was fun, so I played them, even when my wife needed me. This only increased the brokenness in our relationship.

Neither one of us was feeling fulfilled in our marriage, not even with the physical parts. We had barely tipped the scale on our sex life—and hello! We were newlyweds who waited until our wedding night to have sex! Where was all the suspense and excitement? We spent most of our free time separate, with Dino playing video games and me either shopping or thinking about shopping.

We needed help. We were living each day with guns cocked and loaded with plenty of emotional ammo aimed at the other. Dino was distracted all the time, and I was crying every day.

After one of our arguments, I brought up the *c* word: counseling.

Have you ever noticed that as soon as you think you might need counseling and then say it out loud, suddenly everything seems really great? You're like, *Nah, we don't need counseling! I'm fine. We're fine. Everything's fine!* Only to realize a few days later that all your problems are still there and are now even worse?

We made an appointment.

It was another hot day in Vegas when we walked into the counselor's office for the first time. Both of us tried to put on a show with big old smiles pasted on our faces that screamed, "It's all good!" but inside we were kind of dying—and nervous about opening up to a therapist we didn't know.

"So, what brings you here today?" he asked.

I started in, sharing my concerns about how much time Dino spent gaming. "There is just no balance," I said. "It's nonstop. I don't feel seen. What I'm trying to say is I hate video games, and I hate that Dino plays them."

While I was rapid-firing all my cares and woes to the therapist, Dino was loading up his emotional ammo. When it was his turn to share, boy, did he have a lot to say!

"She spends all her time shopping!" Dino said. "She spends so much money—money we don't have. Last Saturday she spent $147 on stuff we don't even need. I want to put her on an allowance."

Eeeech! Slam on the brakes. Hold up, fool! "Allowance"? I am not your child.

No doubt the counselor had faced this type of scene plenty of times before: a couple of young kids who jumped into marriage not knowing a lick about anything. Now they were complaining about video games, shopping, and money. Classic.

I hated the term *allowance*; all it did was fuel an even bigger argument about roles, money, finances, and who was the boss of whom. I believe God designed marriage to be a relationship in which each person loves the other with the kind of love Jesus modeled. It's a sacrificial love that puts the needs of the other person first. But neither one of us understood this yet, nor did we know how to love each other that way.

Our visits with that therapist helped us in two significant ways. First, it validated that Dino's nonstop video-game playing was a problem. "By choosing gaming over time with your wife," the counselor said, "you're communicating clearly that she is not your priority." Dino got it.

Second, it helped me see that my constant shopping was also an issue. I shopped whenever I felt discontent inside, but I came to realize that buying more stuff wouldn't soothe that ache. It was a short-term fix that was killing our finances and making Dino feel completely unheard.

We realized our family needed to be on a budget. And what better way to be sure we stuck to a budget than to put the problem spender in charge of the money? So that's just what we did. I would now be responsible for making sure we were living within our means.

Dino handed over all of the microfinances—the day-to-day bill paying and discretionary spending—to me, and he took care of the macro stuff (such as savings and retirement). Suddenly, I could see how all my "little" purchases added up each month. And oh, man, how our worlds changed! As the strong woman my mama raised, you can bet your bottom dollar I was now watching every penny.

God designed marriage to be a sacrificial love that puts the needs of the other person first.

Gone were my days of buying things on a whim. No more mindlessly spending money on cute pillows at T.J. Maxx. Dino's spending habits changed too. He would often see my phone number pop up on his caller ID shortly after lunchtime.

"Babe, did you just spend ten dollars on a burger?" I'd drill him. "I just logged onto our credit card online, and I see a ten-dollar charge to In-N-Out."

"Busted," he'd say.

"That's three dollars over your lunch budget," I'd tease. "Why are you spending all our money! And in case you're wondering, my homemade tuna sandwich was delicious—and practically free." Hey, if I was going to be in charge of our money, I wanted us to be thrifty.

The tables had turned, but for the better. To this day we handle our finances this way. (Except I've learned to chill out a bit. I don't drill Dino if he orders a burger at lunch.) When one of us overspends, we've learned to discuss it and then make a plan that gets us back on budget.

Once we were doing better with our finances, we fought less over money but soon realized that the demands of Dino's job were taking a toll on our marriage as well. The culture there was fast-paced and high-challenge, which Dino loved. But it seemed there was always a crisis or crash project to manage, which required him to suck it up and work crazy hours.

Even on normal days, he worked long hours at the office in downtown Las Vegas. One evening while I was making dinner, he called.

"Hey, Ash, I have to stay late tonight," he said. "I'll probably be home around ten or eleven."

Blah! I hated those nights. But when there was a deadline, it was crunch time and he had to work as long as he was needed.

"Fine," I said. But I was annoyed.

I went to bed alone, crying again, and woke up the next morning still alone. Next to me was Dino's pillow, but no Dino. I panicked.

Did he not come home? Has he been in an accident? I grabbed my phone and dialed his cell phone, imagining the worst.

"Hey, babe," he said. "I got stuck here all night. Sorry I didn't call, but I didn't want to wake you." He sounded exhausted. I could hear his coworkers talking in the background.

When he got home later that day, we talked. We had been in Vegas for what seemed like an eternity but it had been less than a year. Sure, we were saving money on rent and living in a really nice house. We'd made some good changes in my shopping and Dino's gaming. But we weren't happy with our work-home balance, nor could we ever be as long as Dino was at that job.

The all-nighter at work made it clear: This wasn't the life we wanted. We didn't have kids yet, but it was something we talked about often. We didn't want to live this way, let alone bring a child into a home like this.

Dino updated his résumé and submitted it to a few companies in Southern California. We were taking another step toward improving our marriage.

It worked. A month later, we left Las Vegas for Dino's new job outside Los Angeles, and a new era in our lives began. After ten and a half months, I finally stopped crying.

designing a space
you don't own

During this season, I was trying to figure out who I was—and unfortunately it cost me a pretty penny because I thought I could find my identity through design. I knew I needed to shift more of my focus inward if I wanted to fill the ache I couldn't yet name. I just didn't know where to begin.

Despite the tears, it had been a season of beauty when I'd had the chance to flex some God-given design muscles. Because we were living in a house that didn't belong to us, I wasn't free to paint, change the flooring, or retile the bathroom. I was forced to think outside the box and stretch my creativity whenever I wanted to give a room a different feel. It turns out that while trying to discover myself, I began to uncover my design style simply by experimenting in small ways.

One of the most rewarding temporary updates I've done in our various homes was swapping out the cookie-cutter doorknobs, hinges, and drawer pulls on kitchen and bath cabinets with hardware that showed a hint of my personality. The impact of this simple change was dramatic—and all it took was a screwdriver. Quick and easy.

IDEA 1

IDEA 2

QUICK TIPS

- Collect ideas from Pinterest, Instagram, and other digital media.
- Swap out pillow covers and rugs or experiment with a removable wallcovering.
- Offer to update or improve your space in exchange for a discount in rent from your landlord.

DESIGNING A SPACE YOU DON'T OWN

Live in a rental apartment, house, or dorm? You can still "own" your space by flexing your design creativity through these simple tips:

⋙ **Find ideas on Pinterest or Instagram.** Don't know what your design style is? Experiment! But instead of buying and trying different looks like I did, save yourself the headache and money by hopping on Pinterest or Instagram, where a quick search by room will net you scores of fantastic ideas. Create a board and fill it with design ideas you like. Choose one or two ideas you'd like to copy.

⋙ **Make nonpermanent changes.** There are plenty of things you can do to make your space unique so it feels like home! Think in terms of temporary improvements. Here are some of my favorites:

• **Pillow covers.** Throw pillows will add a pop of color to your bedroom or living space. I like buying pillow covers for pillows I already own because then I can swap them out when I want a different look. Pillow covers are great space savers.

- **Rugs.** Rugs can make a strong design statement and cozy up any room. Don't hesitate to add a rug on top of carpeting. Think in terms of layers and textures that add a designer look to your room.

- **Removable wallcoverings.** Don't have permission to paint? A removable stick-on wallpaper or backsplash is a fun way to spruce up a space without damaging the walls. Time to move? Just peel it off and you're done! Another option: Hang fabric with thumb-tacks to create a contrast wall. A flat sheet with a design or color you love can really brighten up a dreary room or even an office space.

>>> **Appeal to your landlord.** Ask the owner if you can make some approved updates or improvements in exchange for a rental discount. You might not get reimbursed for your labor, but perhaps your land-lord will cover the cost of materials. I know lots of people who've had suc-cess with this approach. The owner gets a "free" update to their property, and you get to flex a little design muscle. Win-win!

03

so much new

No one is ever quite ready; everyone is always caught off guard. Parenthood chooses you.
And you open your eyes, look at what you've got, say "Oh, my gosh," and recognize
that of all the balls there ever were, this is the one you should not drop.

——MARISA DE LOS SANTOS, *Love Walked In*

It felt so great to be back in Southern California. It just felt like home. We moved into a little apartment in Agoura Hills, about forty-five minutes west of Los Angeles. Dino settled into his new job, which had a slightly better work schedule. I began working as a stylist at a hair salon. And eight months into our new life in Southern California, we found out we were pregnant.

Well, what comes with pregnancy (besides nausea and some exhaustion)? Nesting! And oh, man, did I have it bad.

We liked our apartment well enough, but I was itching for a home of our own to bring our sweet baby boy into. Dino crunched some numbers and decided that financially we were ready to buy our first house.

new home

We always joke that I am the gas and Dino is the brakes in our relationship. And with this house search, I had my foot all the way down on that gas pedal. Scouring the competitive California housing market, I was like a hyper, distracted puppy.

"Oh! Oh! Dino, look at this one!" I'd say, pointing to the newest Redfin listing on my laptop screen. "Oh, no—wait! Look at this! Babe, how about this one?"

Dino always had the same answer: "No." I was mostly pointing out houses that were at the very top of our price range, and it made him nervous to be cutting it close. Dino is super responsible when it comes to finances. This was our first home purchase—and it was scary.

> *We always joke that I am the gas and Dino is the brakes in our relationship.*

I wasn't looking at prices or thinking about how large a mortgage we could comfortably afford. I just saw photos of an open layout in a nice neighborhood. *Works for me!* As I'd scroll through photos of each room, my mind would go crazy with all the things I could do with each spot.

And when we visited homes in our price range, no matter the floor plan, I consistently asked one question: "Could we take down that wall?" I just love the openness of a great-room concept. But to our Realtor, it appeared I didn't like walls because I had such a desire to tear them all down.

Dino's constant no to houses I liked was wearing on me, and my unrelenting nagging over each potential house was wearing on him. Despite our agreed-upon distribution of financial responsibilities (me responsible for the day-in, day-out stuff and him for the big-picture stuff), it was clear I didn't trust his judgment on big financial decisions like buying a house. And my second-guessing everything left him feeling disrespected. The more he said no, the more I nagged. The more I nagged, the more he avoided conversations—which led to more badgering and more nos. The house-hunting process brought out the worst in both of us.

Then one day, just three months before our baby was due, we went to look at yet another house—a five-bedroom, 2,800-square-foot home in Moorpark, California, just an hour northwest of Los Angeles. This house had amazing bones, with clearly enough room for our growing family. We were excited to turn a house into our home, and this one was the perfect shade of "ugly and run down" for us to come in and fix up. On our drive home, I finally got a yes from my husband.

This was in 2009, and the housing bubble had just crashed—a heartbreak for many, but for first-time home buyers like us, it was a dream market with lots of affordable options. I planned to quit my job at the salon right before the baby was born, so with only Dino's income to support us moving forward, we had to stretch every penny we had to make it happen. In May we closed on our first home.

Budget, budget, budget. This was Dino's favorite word, and you know what? It had become mine, too! Our ability to work together collaboratively in an area as challenging as finances boosted our confidence in our marriage. I learned to listen to what Dino had to say about money and to treat his ideas with respect rather than resistance and nagging. He learned to relax, trust me, and have a more open mind about the ways I wanted us to invest our money—especially on discretionary expenses like remodeling our outdated new home.

Seriously, this house needed some tender loving care. We gave ourselves a budget to work within and started prioritizing and pricing out each project. Blue carpet covered in stains, moldy showers, and a staircase that clearly wasn't up to code—these were projects we tackled before we moved in. We were able to save a ton of money on necessary improvements because most of the work on the house was done by friends and family. Even so, after covering the necessary upgrades, we didn't have much of a budget left for cosmetic updates.

I had always loved the hunt of a deal, and now I was growing to love the challenge of keeping a balanced budget. I pored over Pinterest and Instagram, looking for ideas for each room in our new home, dreaming of what it could become. Then

I'd challenge myself: *How can I accomplish this same look but stay within my tiny budget?* The challenge! Oh girl, watch out!

The backyard, too, was a hot mess, so we tore it up. By early July, I was nine months pregnant. My dad and Dino installed a sprinkler system—essential for the California heat—while my mom and I planted all the shrubs and flowers in landscape beds. Then, on July 3, we laid sod in our entire backyard. (Yes, I unrolled and laid out sod while nine months pregnant—in a bikini no less, because, well, summer. In California.)

At 6:00 p.m. on July 4, my water broke, and the next day, we welcomed our sweet baby boy Gabriel into the world. He was absolutely perfect, and our lives have never been the same.

new parents

Dino and I still argued about a lot of things, but when it came to parenting, we were pretty much on the same page. We had read a parenting book together during pregnancy. This got us all geared up and ready for babyhood. We were still so young—twenty-six and twenty-two—with minds like sponges. We wanted to do it well—together.

In hindsight, I wish we had taken the book's advice with a grain of salt. Our firstborn got the short end of the stick. We probably could have dialed back the sleep training just a tad. Poor Gabe! We aren't alone; first-time parenting is rough.

One lesson we took away from that book, however, turned out to be of great help. I believe it has been a pillar of strength for our marriage to this day. The authors recommended that the husband-wife relationship remain primary in the family, even in the midst of the all-consuming baby years. While children are a gift to this world and to our lives, they said, they shouldn't become our entire world and run our life. They should be a welcome addition to it—not only for the couple's sake, but for the kids. Children rely on a solid relationship between their parents. It gives them security, so the book advised couples to make the father/mother relationship primary.

No arguments here. That just made sense to us. I think lots of couples struggle with this, but I always suggest that they think back to when they first met. Can they remember those days of crazy-hot chemistry? Remember those two people who vowed to love each other through thick and thin? Yeah, why do we seem to forget those days so easily once babies come along?

Perhaps it's because those newborn days and sleepless nights are both blissful and exhausting. Never had Dino or I known a love like we felt for this little eight-pound baby we'd created together. But at the same time, babies are needy and basically run their parents ragged. We did our best to fully attend to Gabe's physical and emotional needs while still prioritizing our relationship with each other. We wanted to model a healthy relationship to him from day one.

We didn't always get it right. On too many nights, Dino's laptop followed him home and he spent the evenings finishing up work. I was home full time with the baby, and sometimes I was unable to exit "mom zone" and remember who I was as a woman and a wife. But we entered parenthood with a mindset that has served our kids—and ourselves—really well. By prioritizing our marriage, we gave our kids confidence in the strength of our relationships with each of them—and with their parents' love for each other.

Having a baby meant making some necessary changes to our house, especially once Gabe started crawling. As a lover of design, I dove into this fresh challenge. Seeing his toys lying all over the floor stressed me out. I refused to let our home look like a tired Chuck E. Cheese playroom, clearly intended for kids' use only. Instead, I gathered a handful of cute baskets to store Gabe's favorite toys in our living area so he could grab them himself and play. His toys now had their own spots, which were both pretty and functional. Carving out space for his toys made it easy to keep him entertained without robbing our home of its beauty and peaceful vibe.

It wasn't just kid clutter that added stress to my life. I realized that all disorder makes my life more stressful as a mother. I started simplifying things for Dino and me as well. I cleared out a kitchen drawer to hold car keys, sunglasses, pens, and other stuff that gathered on the counter each day. I found a serving tray to use as a shoe caddy, giving our entry a more organized, clean look. And I added a basket at the bottom of the stairs where any of us could place all the little things that needed to get put away upstairs. These small changes helped the house stay clean and made our lives more peaceful.

Sixteen months later, we welcomed our second baby boy, Gavin, to the family. During that newborn era, we were pretty exhausted, like every new parent. But

even on the most overwhelming days, Dino and I continued to make time daily for each other, doing our best to keep the boys in a rhythm that worked for our family.

Once Gavin was sleeping well through the night, we tried to get both boys to bed by seven each evening. I know this bedtime sounds crazy to some, but kids need way more nighttime sleep than we adults sometimes give them.[1] Granted, putting the boys to bed this early meant that they often woke around 7:00 a.m. But the trade-off was well worth it. It gave us our evenings together to connect.

Our roles were pretty traditional back then. Dino focused on crushing it all day at work while I focused on the kids. Once the babies were down at night, we enjoyed "us" time.

Anyone who is the primary caregiver of littles can relate. At some point, adult conversation and companionship are a must. With this schedule in our home, every single evening I had an at-home date night with my husband.

Protecting our evenings for grown-up time was a huge intentional step to prioritize our marriage, and it had a positive impact on our kids as well. There's an old saying: "If Mama ain't happy, ain't nobody happy." For Dino and me, a modified version of this mantra turned out to be true: "If Mom and Dad are happy, the rest of the family is happy." By investing in our marriage every evening, we were filling up our love bank, which then overflowed into our family life. And as a new mom (and the stay-at-home parent), gifting myself with those peaceful evenings of adult conversation and some free time to be creative and do my own thing made me a far better mama—trust me!

new job, same dino

I can't help but reflect on this season of life and see how much we were being molded and shaped. We still had so many things to learn and so much growing to do, but change doesn't happen overnight.

I truly wanted to be a great husband and father. I wanted to love my wife and kids with the kind of love Jesus modeled to His followers—a love that sacrificed itself for others. But I vacillated between wanting to serve my wife and family and wanting to do whatever Dino wanted.

Work was also a huge priority, and my desire to be successful there was insatiable. I wanted to be the best, be seen as the best, and exceed everyone's expectations. We'd moved from Vegas to California, but while our geography had changed, I'd brought my work obsession with me. *Driven* isn't the right word because it's not extreme enough. I was absolutely and completely obsessed with being the best. You can imagine how this played out for Ashley and the boys.

I sensed that God wanted to invite me into something amazing for my relationship with Ash, but I knew it would come at a cost. I would no longer be able to simply check a box when it came to my marriage and family: *Spend time with wife? Check. Play with boys? Check.* To experience the kind of marriage God designed for us, I would need to let Him lead me. No more halfway attempts at relinquishing what Dino wanted. I would need to do what was best for the family.

I wasn't ready to make that sacrifice. I had spent a decade honing my skills as a software engineer, and I really wanted to focus on my career. I wanted to get us to a point where we were financially free, so I could . . . well . . . I hadn't thought that far ahead, but if I could just get us there, I was sure it would be amazing, and my drive to achieve would finally be satisfied.

> *If Mom and Dad are happy, the rest of the family is happy.*

I'd been promoted to lead the technology department for a small company in Hollywood. I was given complete control to decide how the company positioned itself from a technology standpoint, and I was so proud. I was finally in a position of leadership.

This promotion only fed my hunger for success. I would tell everyone my new title, hoping they'd see how talented I was. Let me be clear: I wasn't just *proud* of what I'd accomplished; I was haughty and boastful. I thought I was better than everyone else. It's embarrassing to put these truths in ink, but this is where I was at that point in my life. My poor colleagues! My poor wife!

The days were long. I'd wake up at four every day, drive into the office, work from 5 a.m. until 3 p.m., then drive home and complete my workday on my laptop, where I was semipresent for the family.

Ash and I had been married for six years, we were raising two little kids, and I'd executed every plan I'd set for myself professionally. But inside, I was a mess. I was still obsessed with work at the expense of my family. I wasn't fooling anyone—not Ash, not the kids. They knew where my heart was, and where it wasn't.

new pregnancy

Despite Dino's out-of-balance work life and his growing cockiness around his job, our love for each other was strong. We still fought over the same things that had plagued our marriage since Las Vegas, but overall life was sweet. Some parts of our home life—especially parenting—were actually going really well.

We had planned on having just two kids, so once Gavin was born, we were pretty convinced we were done. Except I didn't feel done. I've always been close with my mom, and I longed for that kind of delightful relationship with a daughter of my own. We decided to go for one more baby.

Dino and I began trying to get pregnant when Gavin was still a toddler. A couple of months later, I bought a pregnancy test. When I saw those two distinct blue lines, I knew: *Pregnant!*

This pregnancy started out like the first two. I was nauseated, tired, and excited to find out the sex of the baby. My first routine doctor's appointment at around seven weeks went great. Our baby looked like a cute little wiggly gummy bear on the ultrasound screen.

This was shaping up to be a textbook Petrone pregnancy: plenty of first-trimester nausea, which I would likely ditch around week fourteen as I'd done with both boys. Then it would be nothing but sunshine, rainbows, and joy.

At around ten weeks I started to feel better. *Woohoo! I guess my body knows what's up this time around. I kicked that sickness early. I'm a tough and tested third-time mom!*

On the morning of my twelve-week OB check, Dino was scheduled to lead a big meeting at work, so my mom accompanied the boys and me to the doctor's office. This would be the first OB appointment Dino had ever missed. Because it was an ultrasound day, I thought it would be fun for the boys to come along so they could see their new sibling on the screen.

The four of us crammed into the tiny office with the doctor, but it was worth it. I lay down on the gurney, and the doctor began moving the ultrasound wand over my belly. Gabe and Gavin, now four and two, watched the screen as our little gummy bear appeared. But after about thirty seconds, the doctor lifted the wand and turned to my mom.

"Can you take the boys out into the waiting room?" he asked.

My heart stopped. I looked at my mom, my eyes filled with fear. She stared back, alarmed, but without skipping a beat, she gathered up the boys and left the room.

The doctor turned to me. "I am so very sorry, Ashley," he said, "but something is wrong."

Tears began streaming down my face. I looked at the screen. *Why am I alone for this? Where is Dino?*

"The baby hasn't grown," my doctor continued, "and I'm so sorry, but there is no heartbeat."

I could see exactly what he was talking about. I was almost twelve weeks pregnant, but my baby still looked like the little gummy bear I had seen a few weeks ago.

I tried to keep it together, but I was a hot mess, barely able to hear what he was saying. *How could I lose a baby? I've had two healthy pregnancies!*

Because it was early enough in my pregnancy, the doctor suggested I let the miscarriage happen at home. He wrote a prescription for the hospital pharmacy that would allow this to happen more rapidly and naturally.

My phone had no signal in the hospital, so I couldn't call Dino right then to tell him the news. This appointment had taken far longer than a routine checkup, and I knew he must be worried.

D I had a big presentation for some out-of-state clients that day. I stayed home from the office and ran the presentation via a videoconference that started around the same time as Ash's appointment. I wasn't worried or distracted since her appointments were always so quick. Plus, she was the picture of good health and seemed to be having another textbook pregnancy.

After the presentation, I cranked out a few post-meeting tasks and then looked down at my watch. It had been two hours since Ash's appointment, and she hadn't called with an update. This wasn't like her. A rush of panic hit.

I grabbed my phone and called her, but it went straight to voice mail. I tried again and again. *No reception? No answer, even after two hours? Is she still at the hospital?*

Finally, my call went through. Ash picked up, but on the other end, I heard only her sobs.

And I knew. Somehow I just knew we'd lost the baby.

"Oh, babe," I said. "I'm so sorry. Come on home. I love you. Just . . . just come on home."

"Babe," was all she could manage to say. And then she simply hung up the phone.

What exactly had happened? And why didn't I go with Ash to that appointment? Why did I make her go through this alone? I felt completely overloaded with guilt.

I didn't know what to do. In shock, I walked into the backyard, fell to my knees on the grass, and began to bawl. Ash and the boys would be home in about fifteen minutes, and I wanted to compose myself before they arrived. I wanted to be strong. I wanted to help our family through this. But all I could do was weep.

Are You kidding me, God? How could this be happening? I was broken.

Then I thought of the baby—our little gummy bear. All our dreams for the future crashed in on me. I would never get to meet this child. The pain was overwhelming.

I was caught up in a hurricane of emotions, slammed over and over again by waves of guilt, anger, frustration, confusion, and sorrow. I hurled unfiltered thoughts and words at God, raw and real. As I lay on my knees crying, I begged God for clarity, for understanding, and for Him to bring healing to us.

And then came an inexplicable sense of peace, as if God met me in the eye of that storm, placed His hand on my back, and just said, "Calm."

Whenever I got hurt as a kid, my dad would hold me and tell me it was going to be okay. That's how this felt. I knew I had a choice in that moment— either to lean toward God or to pull away.

I leaned in. Like a wounded child, I buried my head into God's chest and did my best to surrender everything I was feeling. This miscarriage made no sense to me. It broke my heart. But in those moments before my wife and sons arrived home, I surrendered all my confusion and sorrow to God.

I don't remember the drive home from the hospital. I was numb with shock. My parents were kind enough to take Gabe and Gavin so I could miscarry our sweet baby at home. I'll never forget those few days.

Thus far in our young lives, Dino and I had been protected from significant pain. We'd always felt a little like "golden children"—untouchable, with only small, manageable problems. At some level, we chalked our good fortune up to God. Bad things don't happen to good people, do they? We were faithful, obedient Christians, after all. Why would we experience heartache? And yet we'd just lost our baby.

This isn't how it's supposed to work. We were so confused. *Why would He do this to us?*

Dino and I hunkered down for a few days in our bedroom, which became a haven for us. Snuggled together in bed, we cried, talked, read some comforting words from the book of Psalms in the Bible, watched some of our favorite TV shows, and just . . . waited.

Dino and I didn't talk much. Rather, we just really needed the other's presence, to be in a safe space where we could comfort each other. We prayed together, but beyond that, we didn't really discuss the actual loss too much. We both knew there were just no words.

Losing this baby was the first big loss either of us had experienced. Those days bonded us together at a deeper level. What started out as a time of confusion and heartache turned into a time of reflection and peace. It was truly a gift to be left alone and have the chance to mourn together.

There's something so powerful about experiencing a shared loss. Humans long for authentic connection and comfort in times of sorrow, and that's just what Dino and I experienced—not just with each other, but with God.

It took some heavy-duty wrestling with our feelings, but to the best of our abilities, we surrendered this loss to God. By the time my body said goodbye to the little one we'd already grown to love, our mentality had shifted. What had begun as "Why? Why, God!" progressed to "Thank You, God." *Thank you?* How could we possibly thank God for the loss of a child? We weren't thanking God for the miscarriage itself, but for the fact that no sorrow can put us beyond His ability to care for us, to bring goodness from what seems to be tragic.

Turns out Dino and I are not golden children after all. None of us are. Life isn't perfect. Everyone faces deep loss at some point—the kind that takes our breath away. This doesn't mean we're unloved or alone. God is there with us in our pain. In fact, it's often in those times that He shows up the strongest.

I read a passage of Scripture written by James. I'd read it many times before

Humans long for authentic connection and comfort in times of sorrow, and that's just what Dino and I experienced—not just with each other, but with God.

and probably even memorized it when I was a little girl, but it had new meaning to me in light of our loss:

> Consider it pure joy, my brothers and sisters, whenever you face trials of many kinds, because you know that the testing of your faith produces perseverance. Let perseverance finish its work so that you may be mature and complete, not lacking anything.
> JAMES 1:2-4, NIV

Consider it joy? Seriously? Could I have joy in the midst of heartache? Could I really feel joy and comfort instead of loss and anger? I couldn't imagine. That kind of inner transformation was beyond my ability. And I refused to just fake it, to "make lemonade out of lemons."

Instead, Dino and I asked God together to help us experience that kind of joy—the kind that isn't rooted in happy circumstances and a golden-child life. We prayed that He would give us the peace only He could give, and to grow us in perseverance and maturity.

Losing that little one was the most painful loss I'd experienced—and remains so to this day. I'll always wish we'd welcomed a healthy new baby into our lives at the end of that pregnancy. But from today's vantage point, I am glad I'm no longer a golden child. I'm learning to embrace uninvited loss.

I don't look back with anger at my body or at God. Instead, my memories of those days, lying in bed next to Dino, grieving together, sharing the most intimate of losses together, are among the most beautiful of my life. I will always grieve the loss of our baby, but alongside that, I also feel an overflowing sense of gratitude. I'm thankful that this loss ultimately brought me closer to Christ. I'm thankful for the soul bond that grew between my husband and me during those sorrowful days.

Having experienced the heartache of miscarriage, my capacity for walking alongside others in their pain has grown immensely. On those occasions when Dino or I share our miscarriage experience with others and they find comfort in hearing about our journey, I'm so deeply grateful. God has used that loss for something good.

organized chaos

Life is a mixture of highs and lows, some that are obvious and some that surprise us. The miscarriage, obviously, was a deep, deep low. Welcoming two healthy little boys into our family were huge highs. Buying our first home was also a high point, for sure, especially because it gave the budding designer in me a chance to develop.

The house had wall-to-wall 1980s blue carpet, complete with stains and snags. We ripped out every inch of it and replaced it with new carpet and laminate wood flooring, which made every room look clean and bright. The rooms were painted dark, dingy colors, but a quick coat of Benjamin Moore Revere Pewter paint lightened up the whole place. Using the same color for most walls gave the whole house a more cohesive look and made the rooms feel bigger and more open.

Dino and I had so much fun learning how to budget our projects. We dabbled with a little DIY to make our dollars stretch and help it all come together. Soon we had a welcoming, cozy home that was uniquely us for a fraction of what it would have cost to pay contractors to make these updates. And we had the added satisfaction of having done it ourselves.

Dino loved that house. Being a numbers guy, he knew we'd bought at the right time. This meant he never wanted to move again. Ever.

"Why would we move when we could just stay here and pay off our house at an early age?" he reasoned.

I couldn't fault his logic. We'd made the most out of what this house had to offer, and we'd stuck to our budget. I was so grateful for the roof over my head and the space for our boys to run around. But I'm a creative who loves change—and more specifically, who loves to stretch herself through home design. Which meant that Dino and the kids needed to get used to ongoing renovations.

That era in our first home turned out to be a great season of personal growth for me. I learned how to renovate a home with two little boys underfoot. I learned I didn't need to wait for the perfect house or the perfect timing in our family's life to find joy in everyday moments. Rather than dreaming about the next home or the next season, I was honing my design skills and learning to embrace the organized chaos of life with toddlers.

managing remodel chaos

Remodeling is messy and chaotic—not exactly conducive to a peaceful home. But you can still find joy in the midst of the mess. Dino and I both tend to thrive in organized chaos (key word: *organized*). In our first house (and the homes we've bought and remodeled since), I learned a few tricks that keep the disarray manageable during a remodel.

BEFORE

AFTER

QUICK TIPS

▶ Keep materials tidy, cleaning up at end of day.
▶ Give yourself grace during remodeling chaos.

▶ Barter with friends for what you need.
▶ Go on mini-outings for peace and perspective.

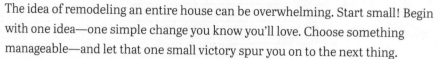

Little Projects with Big Impact

The idea of remodeling an entire house can be overwhelming. Start small! Begin with one idea—one simple change you know you'll love. Choose something manageable—and let that one small victory spur you on to the next thing.

Here are some easy wins that can spark your inspiration and give you the confidence to tackle even greater improvements to the place you call home:

> **Paint an accent wall.** Choose a trendy shade you love and spice up the wall of one room with a little color.

> **Paint a bathroom.** It's small and won't take long. Then buy a shower curtain and towels to match your new color scheme.

> **Redesign and organize your pantry space** with cute labels, baskets, jars, and shelving. Thrift shops are a great source of attractive, affordable containers.

> **Apply peel-and-stick wallpaper** to a wall or backsplash.

> **Buy an area rug** you can layer over existing flooring to cover a tired carpet, or to add color or texture to the room.

> **Paint a piece of wood furniture** a fun color to make it a focal point of the room.

> **Buy a cozy slipcover** to put over your worn sofa.

> **Replace the hardware knobs and drawer pulls** on your kitchen or bathroom cabinets for a fresh look at a fraction of the cost of replacing the cabinets.

> **Remove those heavy, outdated window dressings** to let natural light flood your room. Replace with a light valance, sheer panels—or no curtains at all!

MANAGING REMODEL CHAOS

>>> **Keep it tidy.** With little ones underfoot, I learned quickly that staying on top of the mess was key to maintaining my sanity. I disciplined myself to bring each project to a stopping point at the end of the day, even if I wasn't finished. I put away whatever tools I was done using, cleaned my paintbrushes, added any needed items to my shopping list, and reset the project to be continued the next day.

This habit meant that I went to bed with a sense of satisfaction for the day's accomplishments and that each morning our family awoke to a peaceful home.

>>> **Give yourself grace.** This is a big one. Early on, I would often feel defeated by my inability to both remodel a home and entertain as if my kitchen were not torn apart into a million pieces, with only a microwave plugged into a hallway outlet for cooking. One day on the phone, my mom challenged me on the expectations I was putting on myself.

"Ashley," she said, "you are raising two little kids, your house is a minefield of remodeling debris, and you're hosting three couples for dinner. C'mon! Cut yourself some slack!

No one will mind if your dinner isn't fancy. They just want to be with you. Order out! Eat on your laps! No one will mind."

She was right. Our friends totally understood. "To be honest," one of the wives told me, "if you'd gone all fancy on us in the middle of this demolition zone, we would have to hate you. So thanks for being human."

Think of your current state of chaos as a gift to your friends. It shows you're human—and gives them permission to be human too. Remind yourself that it's okay if everything isn't perfect. Who cares, really, if you're eating off paper plates or washing your dishes with the hose outside? (Yep. Done that.) The kids will be okay. Everyone will live. And remember: You're building your family's history. Those crazy things you did to survive the chaos are becoming part of your collective story. You're creating memories your kids will never forget.

>>> **Barter with friends.** If a remodel affects critical basic functions in your house (think laundry, showering, and cooking), get creative and come up with a win-win trade with friends or family.

- **Swap laundry for a meal.** Ask a friend if you can bring over a meal (or a bottle of wine) and then throw a couple of loads of your dirty clothes in their washer. Add in some good convo once you're there, and it's basically a great date!
- **Trade babysitting for a day away.** Offer to watch your friend's kids for the day (or evening) while you enjoy the relative peace and quiet of their home (and time away from the drywall dust and construction noise at your place).

>>> **Go on mini-outings.** During renovation, plan a few outings with the fam. Take dinner to the park or spend the night at the grandparents' house. Stepping away—if only for a few hours—will give you a little peace and a fresh perspective.

04

hobby jobby

If by "plans" you mean waiting by the door while my three-year-old
puts on his own shoes, then yeah. I have plans today.

----ATTRIBUTED TO THE 21ST CENTURY STAY-AT-HOME MOM

The next few years were a blur. I mean, I had two boys sixteen months apart. Poor Gavin has no baby pictures because I was so busy chasing Gabe—a very strong-willed toddler. I had quit my job as a hairstylist and was a full-time mommy. My days were full, for sure, but I was hankering for one more baby. I still wanted a daughter.

We began trying for another baby as soon as I healed from our miscarriage. When we saw two distinct lines appear on a pregnancy test again, we were thrilled.

The early weeks of that pregnancy were unnerving. Again and again, I reminded myself of all God had taught me through the heartbreak of our last pregnancy. I knew no matter what the outcome, we'd get through it. But, of course, I longed to hold a new baby in my arms.

When we crossed the twelve-week mark, Dino and I both began to breathe a little easier. And as a bonus, we discovered this baby was indeed a girl—a daughter.

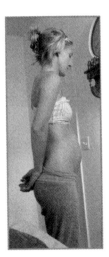

 When Ash got pregnant again, we knew this would be our third and final kid, and this time we were having a girl.

I was about a year into my tenure at the Hollywood company where I worked, and despite my desire to maintain balance in my life and put my family first, I was no closer to being the dad or husband I knew I should be. Same song, third verse. Not much had changed since Vegas. I was still living for Dino. I was spending way too much time playing video games or working overtime. I was also neglecting my fitness and time with my family. My life was out of balance at every angle.

Ashley's labor with this baby, like that of the boys, was uncomplicated, and Quinn was born as I held Ash's hand. Mama and baby were healthy. The nurse scooped up our daughter so she could clean and swaddle her while the doctor attended to Ash. After Mama and Quinn bonded over first-time nursing, Ash turned to me.

"Want to hold your daughter?" She lifted the tiny bundle up to me. I lifted Quinn into my arms and caressed her tiny face.

As soon as I looked into Quinn's eyes, something changed in me. This baby had the largest, most penetrating eyes I've ever seen on a child. It was as if she were peering straight into my soul. I don't know if it was a father/daughter thing or the fact that, since she was my third child, I was a little less nervous around newborns, but as I held her that first time, an insanely overwhelming feeling of love washed over me. It was like nothing I'd ever experienced.

After the births of our boys, it had taken me a little while to feel comfortable and attached to them, but not with Quinn. She looked right into my eyes and owned me. It was as if she saw the many ways I was falling short as a dad, husband, and coworker. As I gazed at her, I wanted to do better, to *be* better. I wanted to be the kind of family man I'd been sensing God created me to be.

A thousand thoughts and memories flashed through my mind. Leading up to Quinn's birth, I had felt increasingly stressed, exhausted, and angry all the time. Though I poured myself into my work, I was sick and tired of my job, and I hated waking up in the morning. Technically, I was doing everything right at home, too: I was there, I was faithful to my wife, I showed up at dinnertime. But I wasn't *really* there. I was grumpy with the kids; my marriage wasn't all that Ash and I wanted it to be. I wasn't making my family a priority. They were just another add-on to *The Dino Show*.

To top it off, I was out of shape physically. I had put on weight. I wasn't exercising. My health was just not a priority, and I didn't see how my indifference around fitness was affecting my mood and energy when I was with my family. My priorities were all still based around what I wanted, what I needed, or whatever I thought would make me feel happy—but I was miserable.

And yet right in the midst of all of it, God gifted me with this baby girl. When looking into her quiet, dark eyes, I saw my life more clearly. I realized everything I had worked for up until this point had been for me. I got married for me; I moved us to Vegas for me; I set aside savings for me; I worked hard at my career for me; I used my free time for me. And I'd learned that living for myself didn't satisfy.

It's fascinating, really. It defies logic. You'd think living for yourself would pay nicely, and outwardly it does, in the short term. We were doing well financially, and I was on track to become exactly what I'd dreamed: powerful, revered by those around me, and wealthy. And yet I had hit the lowest time of my entire life.

> *Living for myself didn't satisfy.*

I was done. I had said this before—I'd even left jobs to try to find the balance I wanted. But the problem wasn't the jobs. The common denominator was me. I was the one who needed to change.

I cradled my new daughter in my arms and kissed her tiny nose. *This time— this time—I must change.*

Shortly after Quinn came home from the hospital, I headed into work one day at 4:30 a.m. Before anyone else arrived, I sat staring at a blank white wall in my office. I thought of all the things I had been living for and imagined prioritizing them on that wall, top to bottom. I remembered all the prayers I'd prayed, asking God to help me be a better husband and dad, despite being unwilling to change at my very core. As I sat there, I sensed God asking me, *How is that working for you?*

I had to admit: *Not so great.* I hated living for myself. I hated who I had become and the person my family had to deal with. I hated that they got only the leftover energy after I had used up my prime time on myself.

It was as if God was inviting me into a different mindset: *Want to try it My way now?*

Sitting alone in my office at the dawn of a new day, I broke down crying. *Okay. Let's try it Your way, God.*

I wasn't sure where to begin. For starters, I decided to start getting up before the kids and begin my day by journaling, praying, and reading passages from the Bible. I wanted to get centered and connected with God before anyone else was awake.

This alone made a big difference. I didn't change magically overnight—I had spent thirty years of my life living for myself, after all. But I was serious about living the rest of my life for something bigger than myself, and this was a good start.

Adjusting to life with three kids took some time. They now outnumbered Dino and me, and I had begun homeschooling Gabe, which took time and planning. But this wasn't our first rodeo, and within a few months I once again found myself in a comfortable rhythm, evenings protected to connect with Dino and give myself some much-needed grown-up time for creativity or fun.

I didn't plan to go back to work in a hair salon after Quinn was born. I loved momming full time, and I also wanted to continue stretching my love of design. One day I was browsing through Craigslist when I came across a dining table I knew was way underpriced. This brand-name piece was solid wood—not veneer—and would sell for at least four figures in a store. All it needed was some love and a little elbow grease.

By the time Dino got home from work, I had bought the table, picked it up from the owner, and begun stripping away the old finish with an electric sander. Within two days—during naptimes and after the kids went to bed—I'd completely removed the old, dated finish; given it a final sanding; applied a light stain that accented the gorgeous wood grain; and applied a few coats of Polycrylic finish to protect the surface from my preschoolers.

As I stood back and admired the finished product, I had a deep sense of satisfaction. In just a few hours, I'd given this beautiful piece a new lease on life, and I knew I could turn around and sell it for ten times what I'd paid. *Wow. There is money to be made here. And it's fun!*

And that's how I picked up a little "hobby jobby"—you know, a hobby that turns into making money! I started buying more pieces of used furniture from Craigslist or at yard sales, refinishing them, and then selling them for a profit. I'd hunt for high-end brands, great deals, and one-of-a-kind vintage items. Whenever I found a new piece to buy, I'd pile the kids into our SUV, and we'd go pick it up. It was an adventure. I've always been a go-go-go mom, and my kids came along for the ride.

Once I got a new piece home, I'd sand it down, repaint or stain it, and then resell it. This work meshed well with my main job of being a mom because it was so flexible. I could work on refinishing furniture during the kids' naps and in the evenings.

Refinishing quality furniture satisfied my itch for design and fed my creativity. It was a messy hobby, but the profit margin was there—and I loved it. Dino, however, was a little slow to jump on board. He mostly saw the mess, and not the profit. One day he came home to find not one but two used dining room tables in our kitchen.

"Are you kidding me? Another table?" he said, pointing to my latest find. "But you just bought that first one last week!"

"Babe, I bought that table for thirty dollars, and I just sold it for three hundred dollars. New owners are picking it up tomorrow."

"Three hundred dollars?" he asked. "For a thirty-dollar table?" I could see his financial wheels calculating the margin of profit.

"Yeah, it's really helping me keep us on budget," I added. *His favorite word. Ha!*

"Um, yeah . . . keep on going, babe," he said. "Don't stop what you're doing. Good job!" (*Insert "jobby."*)

I bought and sold a total of eight tables while living in our Moorpark house—and I didn't stop there. I picked up coffee tables and other items I could resell for a profit.

For someone who loved to work hard, it was exhilarating. I was a stay-at-home mom doing something new that I loved.

Several years into motherhood, if someone asked, "And what do you do?" I'd reply, "I'm a stay-at-home, homeschooling mom." I hadn't really had the time or put any effort into figuring out who I was yet, and I had little spare energy for it anyway. But my desire to find my purpose never went away.

I was constantly praying (aka nagging) that God would give me something more. I loved my kids, and they kept my days filled. I chose to homeschool them, but still I wanted more.

I was learning to wait. *Yuck!* Patience and waiting? Not a fan. "Now" sounds like much more fun! But thankfully God knew what I needed. I stopped badgering Him to give me something more and just asked for His direction and timing. When I did, I found peace in the waiting.

a little idea

I bided my time for a few more years. Then one day I had an idea.

I love home design, deal finding, and furniture refinishing. People always told

> *I stopped badgering God to give me something more and just asked for His direction and timing. When I did, I found peace in the waiting.*

me I had a gift for it and would often compliment me on my home when they came over. Could I possibly share that passion with others?

The possibility that I could help others create beautiful spaces in their homes thrilled me. It was like I had this huge secret and wanted to tell everyone! Could I blog about it? Could I show photos and tell stories on Instagram?

Then fear kicked in. I wasn't trained as an interior designer. I was just a stay-at-home, homeschooling mom. Who was I to share my ideas with the world? And who would want to read anything I wrote?

One day I met with a family friend, Donna, whom I consider a mentor and who has a gift for speaking truth and life into others. I described my "secret" to her—that by sharing my love of design, I could show others how to bring the beauty of good design into their own spaces and homes.

"Donna, I sort of sense I should do this," I said, "but I don't even know where to begin. And who would want to listen to me anyway?"

She looked at me for a moment, thinking. Then she spoke. "Ashley, you have to do this. Honey, you have a gift for creating beauty in your home and inspiring others to do the same. If you are authentic and stay true to yourself, people will love you for it. That's appealing! People are looking for that. I think God gave you something special that's worth sharing—not just your design abilities, but your life. And I think you should share it. Just be yourself."

That was it. The way she put it was so simple. Straight and to the point. *Be myself? Okay. I can do that.*

I now knew a bit of who God had made me to be, and what a great way to figure out who "me" really was. And if people didn't like me, that was okay too. I had always been way too caught up in what others thought about me. But why? Did I really care if someone didn't like me? My worth wasn't in the eyes of others; it was found in the eyes of God. Since He's the one who made me, only His opinion counts!

My fears chilled a bit. *Okay, I can do this!*

I woke up the next day filled with a burning passion and fire to start a blog and an Instagram account that shared simple, doable design tips and ideas—the sorts of projects anyone could do and be successful. I had zero knowledge of websites or social media, but I was married to a tech guy, so . . .

 I was all in. Ash had so much wisdom, skill, and personality to share with the world, and I was thrilled to see her make this investment in herself. She created the name *Arrows and Bow* after our kids: two arrows for our sons and a bow that tied them together for our daughter. I set up her Instagram account and created a WordPress blog for her, and that was that. She was off and running.

My first blog post was titled "Me Doing Me."[2] It was about obedience in waiting as I sorted out whether my love for change and "the hunt" (looking for beauty in home design) could fit into God's purpose for my life. I'd spent years questioning myself and living through the blur of early parenthood, and now I was finally moving out of the fog to see what God had waiting for me.

Little did I know that by starting my blog, I was beginning something that would change me and our family forever.

refinishing furniture
to keep or sell

Remodeling and designing our Moorpark home on a budget was an incredible challenge. So how did I turn our blue-carpeted, moldy-shower house into a home? I focused first on the areas I knew needed updating: the kitchen, bathrooms, that nasty carpet, and a few safety hazards.

Our budget was tight, but the kitchen—a big-ticket item in the world of home remodeling—really needed an upgrade. We couldn't afford to rip out the floors or replace the backsplash. We realized that we could do something about one of the room's focal points: the cabinets. They were solid, but man, were they ugly! Instead of ripping them out and buying new ones, we repainted the cabinets and then rubbed them lightly with stain to give them an antique look. (I was in a French country phase.) Adding new hardware to the doors totally transformed the kitchen. By working within our means and tackling projects we could do ourselves rather than hiring them out, we made our kitchen look brand-new.

I really loved that kitchen because we did it ourselves—and on budget. I also kept hunting for garage-sale deals and making a profit by selling furniture I'd refinished. The money I earned went toward the next home project.

It felt good to know I was working hard and saving for each project. I was earning each improvement. It fueled my drive and gave me greater appreciation for every update.

Refinishing Furniture and Cabinetry

Refinishing quality pieces of used furniture can add beauty to your home—and money to your pocket through resale. As I continued to seek out underpriced, quality furniture, I learned more about appraising pieces and figuring out their age. I once stumbled across a quirky little end table on Craigslist that I immediately recognized as being very old—like, maybe Civil War era. The table was located in a small town several hours away, and it needed refinishing, but it was a true one-of-a-kind find that I couldn't pass up. The owner was selling it for under a hundred bucks, and I knew it was worth far more. The resale potential was high, so I made the trek.

With a treasure like that, I really didn't want to ruin its gorgeous, ancient patina with a shiny-new finish. I made a few small repairs to the hardware, gave it a light sanding where needed, and added tung oil, a natural preservative that would protect the old wood. I originally bought the piece to resell, but I fell in love with it and decided to keep it. It added a unique, serene beauty to our family room, where I placed it against a large window with a vase of dried flowers on top.

QUICK TIPS

▶ Buy quality brands.
▶ Use specific terms to narrow your search when shopping for deals online.
▶ Carefully assess what a piece really needs before starting a complete overhaul.
▶ See what similar pieces are going for and price your item appropriately.

REFINISHING FURNITURE TO KEEP OR SELL

Here are tips for finding neglected or outdated treasures and restoring them to beauty.

⋙ **Know your brands.** Look for brands that hold their value, like Restoration Hardware, Pottery Barn, West Elm, and classic brands like Ethan Allen or Thomasville. You can find quality pieces from these companies at garage sales, estate sales, or resale shops. Type these brand names into your online searches as well.

⋙ **Use key words in your search.** When searching for a desk on Craigslist or other online sites, don't just search for *desk*. If you're looking for a French-style desk, type in words like *French*, *French desk*, *rustic*, *vintage desk*, *old desk*, *wood desk*, or even *French provincial*. It's amazing how a one-word change in your search can yield different results.

⋙ **Don't go overboard.** Not every treasure you find needs a complete overhaul. One-of-a-kind pieces are special because of their uniqueness, and they don't always require a total refurb job. They just need a little sanding and a touch-up. I slow my roll before diving in so I don't completely ruin something that was almost everything it needed to be. If all it needs is a little buffing, you're good to go!

⋙ **Check the market.** Before you list your refurbished treasure for resale, do a quick search online to see what similar items are selling for. You want to be competitive but not underpriced. Make sure you're not giving away your great find—and the time and sweat equity you invested—for free. You can always lower the price if it doesn't sell, but start with solid, competitive pricing.

05

a seismic shift

Discipline is choosing between what you want now, and what you want most.

—ATTRIBUTED TO ABRAHAM LINCOLN

Three babies, eight years of marriage, and a home big enough for us all—we were a happy family of five. From the outside, life appeared pretty dang great. But what was happening inside? What was really going on behind those walls? Shortly after Quinn was born, my brother, Ryan, returned home from the Air Force after a ten-year run of service to our country. Having enlisted right after high school, he had left as a boy and come back a man.

The first time I saw him, I was shocked. "Ry!" I said, hugging him. "Look at your muscles! You're huge!"

He grinned. "I guess they work us pretty hard in the Air Force."

Ryan had always been a fit guy, but the Air Force had done him well. He had become a devout student of the human body and anything to do with physical fitness—and it showed.

Dino took note. He'd once had that same drive, but somewhere along the line he seemed to have lost it. He no longer ran marathons as he had when we first met. He had stopped working out. He had grown a little soft around the middle. He didn't have the same energy he'd once had—though he still had plenty of stamina for playing video games from our sofa! I could tell he was self-conscious about his own fitness as compared to my brother's.

 I had just turned thirty when Ryan came home from the Air Force. The obvious difference between us—not just his fitness level but his remarkable discipline—rattled me. Ever since Quinn was born, I had really wanted to make changes as a dad and husband. But I lacked the self-control. In many ways, I was still acting like a child.

I recalled an insightful perspective I'd read from the apostle Paul: "When I was a child, I spoke like a child, I thought like a child, I reasoned like a child. When I became a man, I gave up childish ways."[3] I wanted to give up my old childish habits, but I didn't know where to begin.

To make matters worse, I had been reinforcing Dino's childlike behavior by acting like his mother. I was constantly saying the same things he'd likely heard from his parents when he was a kid:

"Clean up after yourself!"

"Stop playing video games!"

"Why don't you help out more?"

For lack of a better term, I was a nag. I was constantly trying to fix him, change him, mold him. Whenever I got after him, he would dig in his heels and focus even more on whatever it was he wanted to do. I would pester him some more, and he would push me further away, and around and around we would go. It was a super dysfunctional dance. We each knew our dance steps to perfection, and I realized we wouldn't grow any closer in our marriage until we whipped this parent-child relationship. I had no clue how to break out of this unhealthy pattern.

For the past few years, I had been attending a women's Bible study taught by a wise woman named Chelsea, whom I really respected. Those weekly gatherings were a great way to meet other women and get out of the house. We covered topics like parenting, marriage, and navigating life as a Christian woman.

One week, the teacher discussed a book she had read.[4] The book's author talked about the importance of not only loving our spouses, but truly cherishing them.

I loved Dino, but did I "cherish" him? As Chelsea continued to speak, I realized I was neglecting a key part of my role in our marriage. Because Dino's faults were more outward and visible than mine, I had been focusing on how much he needed to change while conveniently ignoring my own shortcomings—which were many. How easy it is to see the faults of others without taking time to look in the mirror. (Anyone with me on this?)

My eyes were opened in class that day. Chelsea didn't pull any punches. She gave it to us straight: "Stop trying to change your husband, ladies. It is not your job to fix him. And when you nag and interfere, you're actually getting in the way of what God might be trying to work in his life. How about we just focus on changing ourselves? That's a plenty big enough job for each of us."

Gulp. I sank down in my chair.

This was so me. For the entire eight years of our marriage, I had been a consistent nag and irritant to my husband. I justified it by telling myself he needed my guidance. I was just being helpful, right?

Poor Dino! No wonder he was so obsessed with being successful and admired at work. He got little respect or appreciation at home. He was married to a woman whose constant pestering made him feel like everything he did was wrong. I saw clearly how I was getting in the way—not just of what God might want to do in Dino's life, but also of how the two of us might grow as a couple.

"To truly cherish your husband," Chelsea continued, "be intentional about your thoughts toward him. When you look at him, do you mentally pick him apart? Or do you choose to focus on what's good about him? Find the things you adore and fill your thoughts with those things—and then tell him! Speak those things out loud. I'm not saying you never discuss problems, but the problems shouldn't take up all your brain space.

"If there is any kind of abuse going on in your marriage, that's a different story," she added. "Get help, women! Don't tolerate harmful treatment or patterns! But for most situations, you can change the entire dynamic of your marriage by focusing on what you cherish about your husband and giving voice to it."

Her counsel sounded so simple, but it was completely counter to how I'd been viewing and treating my husband. I thought back to the previous afternoon. When I'd heard Dino's car pull into the driveway after work, I'd met him at the door—not with a kiss but with a list. "Hey, babe, the plumber needs you to call him about the shower drain. The replacement grate is out of stock. Oh, and the blinds in the bedroom got delivered, but they're the wrong color. They sent Sandalwood, not Aspen like we ordered." *Ouch.*

Every day was the same. When Dino got home after a long day, I would greet him with, "Hey, you forgot to make the bed this morning. Is that still your chore, or do you want me to just take it over for you?" or "Where's the milk I asked you to pick up? Did you forget? Again?" I made it clear in no uncertain terms what a disappointment he was. *Ugh. What must that feel like?*

What if instead, I greeted him with love? What if I just focused on what I *cherish* about him? What if the first thing he heard when he walked in the door was, "Hello, handsome! How was your day?" How might that change our dysfunctional dance?

Chelsea concluded with a final challenge. "I guarantee you, ladies, you have the power to make significant changes in your relationship—and it begins by simply changing how you think. You have the ability to lift up your husband by turning your thoughts toward what you love about him. Those thoughts become words, the words become actions, and your spouse will feel loved. It will change your pattern."

It will change our pattern? I straightened up in my seat. Suddenly I was

> *You can change the entire dynamic of your marriage by focusing on what you cherish about your spouse and giving voice to it.*

on fire to practice what I had just learned. I wanted to start cherishing my husband—like, now!

I sneaked my phone out of my purse and texted Dino a sweet, spicy message: "I love you so much and I can't wait to see you tonight . . . ;)" And right there in the middle of Bible class, I typed out a few other details about said night's plans. (I'll let you use your imagination!)

And let me just say, Dino was a fan.

D When Ash came home from her women's group that day, she walked into my home office where I was taking a work break—aka playing videos games. *Busted.* She'd caught me goofing off during the middle of the workday, and I knew instantly where this was going. So much for the spicy text she'd sent.

I took a deep breath, bracing myself for a lecture.

It never came.

Instead, she bent down and gave me a kiss. "Love you, babe," she said. "Can't wait for tonight." Then she turned and walked out.

Wait, what?! What just happened? She'd clearly seen me playing video games, but she didn't get mad. She didn't nag or criticize. She didn't say a word. *She's up to something, I know it. I bet she went shopping today and bought something over budget, and now she feels guilty. She's just sucking up.* I quickly forgot about it and moved on.

girls' night out

Now that I'd become aware of how and why my thoughts toward Dino were a huge part of the problem, I began to spot how often my ugly thoughts turned into words.

One place where I noticed this was in my girlfriend groups. I mean, who doesn't love a good girls' night out, am I right? I'd often meet up with the ladies, and we'd gather around, eating, drinking, laughing, and sharing stories of our home lives.

I had already made a conscious decision to work on how I viewed and spoke about Dino. On one particular night shortly after I'd made that shift, the ladies got on the topic of our husbands and sex lives while I was busy stuffing my face with chips and guac.

Now, I'm no prude. Wanna talk about sex? Sure. No problem. But the conversation took a turn real fast into a husband-bashing fest. I felt this sick pit in my stomach and didn't know what to do. No way was I joining in, but I couldn't just sit there and be the only one who wasn't knocking her man. Nor did I want to be a spectator as these women tore into their husbands, many of whom were my friends. If I just sat there in silence, they might think I was trying to act better than everyone else or assume I thought I had the perfect husband.

It was awkward as heck. I made an excuse to leave early and headed for my car. I called Dino on the way home and told him what had happened. Then I just sat there and bawled my eyes out.

"I felt so sick about what they were saying," I said, "maybe because I could relate—because I, too, have done that kind of thing to you in the past. Maybe that's why it hurt so bad. Dino, I am so, so sorry. I don't ever want to be that kind of partner to you, not ever again. Can you ever forgive me?"

"Babe, it's all right," he said. "I know you love me. But thanks for not joining in this time! Not sure I want our sex lives floating out there in the shark tank on open-feeding night."

He made me laugh. But the conviction I felt held true. I had often been tempted to join in the past—usually when I was trying to fit in or feeling sorry for myself and wanting a little sympathy. When I was feeling negative toward my husband, it felt good to sit around and bash someone else for a change.

Not a pretty sight. I wasn't having it anymore, or at least I was making a conscious effort to steer clear of the shark tank.

 In the days and weeks that followed, it was as if Ash had flipped a switch. She stopped trying to be my mom. I could feel her release control.

And it was absolutely terrifying.

Whoa, whoa, whoa. You mean you're not going to nag me anymore? You're not going to try to push me down a certain path? I can drive my own life—and you won't try to grab the steering wheel every two seconds?

Well, crap. If Ashley wasn't going to be the parent in our relationship, that meant I needed to become an adult.

We never had an actual conversation about this shift in how we related, but if we had, it would have sounded something like this.

Ash: You can run your life. I'm gonna stop trying to run it for you. You want to play video games during the workday? Okay. I'm not your mom. I trust you to figure out your priorities.

Me: Seriously?

Ash: Yep. And you know what else? We need your influence and your leadership in our family. I'm done nagging you about how to be a better husband or dad. It's on you now. We need you. I need you. I believe in you. I know that you have our family's best interests at heart. I have your back.

Me: Um, okay. But if you're not going to be telling me what to do, that means I need to actually pay attention. I don't want to make a wrong turn or get us lost.

Ash: That's up to you. Run it. You're a grown man. I trust you to decide what to do, and I'm excited for where you want us to go.

Ash knows I love a good challenge, so this strategy worked brilliantly with how I'm wired. *Okay! Let's do this!*

Since the first time I'd held Quinn in the hospital, I'd been telling Ashley I wanted to make changes in my life. This was my chance. *What do I want our family to look like in five, ten, or twenty years? What do I want my marriage to look like? And how do we get from here to there?*

Over the next week, I took inventory of all the things that currently filled my days. Wow—so many hours were still spent on Dino-centric stuff that didn't get me any closer to what I truly wanted in life. It was time to put away those childish things. I was long overdue to put my family ahead of myself.

I decided to stop all my self-focused hobbies—even my endless obsession with video games. Instead, I began spending more intentional time with my wife, trying to put her needs before my own. Ash loves taking walks in the evening, and I began initiating those walks, even if I was whipped and would rather sit on the sofa with the Xbox controller in my hands. I began taking her out to restaurants more frequently because I know how much she loves to eat

good food with a side of good conversation. These were just small changes, really, but they were tangible things I knew Ash would like that demonstrated a shift in my habits and priorities.

I also invested more quality time in my kids—not just in small, practical ways like helping with bath time or reading to them at bedtime, but in ways that cost me more because they didn't necessarily fit my wiring. Spending a Saturday morning building LEGOs with Gabe wouldn't knock anything off my to-do list. It wouldn't help me conquer any goals or win any points at work. But it accomplished something even more important: It demonstrated to my son that he was valued and loved. He wasn't an afterthought. He was a priority worth investing in.

These changes didn't happen overnight. In fact, they're still in process. I fall back into my childish ways sometimes. But I quickly discovered how much I love investing in my family. And when it comes to living like a responsible grown-up, I don't go it alone. I continue my rhythm of starting my day with solitude, prayer, and journaling. In those early-morning hours, I sense God guiding me.

Dino and I both began starting our days with some quiet time with God. Lasting change doesn't happen overnight, and I knew I needed help to break my habit of nagging. Those times of stillness definitely helped me keep my focus on loving Dino rather than pestering him. Whenever I was tempted to criticize him, I tried to pray for him instead, asking God to grow our marriage and change both our lives.

Certain topics still set me off, however. One was Dino's health. He used to love running, but for the past few years he'd been so stressed about work and the kids that he'd stopped running or working out. Video games didn't help. I mean, who has time for a workout when you need to run that four-hour raid on *World of Warcraft*? Priorities, people!

I've never been one to hold back about what I really think. My mama raised up a strong woman—and let me tell you, I'm no mouse. For sure, Dino already knew how I felt about his gaming habit. But in this new day, I was committed to focusing on what I loved about him rather than picking him apart. I had to let the whole gaming thing go and allow Dino to figure it out in his own way.

There was a seismic shift in each of us, and in our relationship. We could all feel it—even the kids. Learning to "cherish" Dino didn't mean I became mute about issues that needed a little straightforward convo. It tortured me sometimes when Dino did something truly nag-worthy (my definition of *nag-worthy* was still pretty tight). But now, instead of stuffing frustrations, I learned to change my approach. I'd come at him with a soft, gentle spirit; share my thoughts about the issue; and then we'd talk about it. If he chose to see things my way and make a change, great! But if not, it was no longer my job to change him. Actually, it had never been my job, and now my focus was on changing me—how I viewed my husband, how I spoke of him, and how I spoke to him.

The better I got at releasing Dino to be his own grown-up, the less he said no to every suggestion I made. I could tell he felt liberated—as if for the first time since we got married, he could breathe.

> *In this new day, I was committed to focusing on what I loved about him rather than picking him apart.*

I woke up one morning and fumbled down our long staircase in my pajama pants with the goal of getting my morning coffee. Barefoot, I stepped on a loose LEGO, which gouged into my foot. "Gabe! Gavin!" I snapped. "How many times have I told you to put away your dang LEGOs?"

The boys, snuggled into the sofa watching cartoons, looked up, startled by my outburst.

"Sorry, Dad," Gabe said, hurrying to pick up the stray brick.

I felt a twinge of guilt for my overreaction.

At the bottom of the stairs, I caught my own reflection in the hallway mirror. I barely recognized the man looking back at me. *What has become of the Dino I used to be?*

For much of my twenties, I had treated my body like garbage, and it was starting to show. As I entered my thirties, I was starting to gain weight and lose energy. I constantly felt tired and needed way too many naps. With a family history of high blood pressure, heart disease, obesity, and diabetes, I wasn't heading down a good path.

More concerning was my mental state. In the past year or so, I'd found myself increasingly angry, irritable, and moody, which worried me because I have a strong family history of struggles with emotional and mental health as well. Just two hops up my family tree—in my parents' and grandparents' generations—alcoholism, bipolar disorder, depression, Alzheimer's disease, and Parkinson's disease had wreaked havoc on loved ones. Many of these conditions show a strong genetic component, and that frightened me. Was this what my future held? Could I stop it?

Looking at myself in the mirror that morning, I knew more change was needed. I needed to do what I could to protect my brain and my mental health as I got older. If the cards were going to be stacked against me genetically, I needed to do everything I could now to increase the odds of keeping my brain healthy. I wanted to get my health in order and start taking care of my body.

Dino came home from work one day bursting at the seams to tell me some news.

"Ash! I had lunch with Ryan, and guess what? I'm gonna teach your brother how to write software code and hopefully get him an internship at work," he said. "And in exchange—this is the best part—he's gonna train me at the gym! The guy's a beast! I want that! And what do you think about letting him move in with us until he finds a job?"

I couldn't believe my ears. Dino was initiating plans to focus on his health—without me badgering him! Best news ever. *Okay, Ashley, okay. Play it cool. Don't let Dino know this is exactly what you've been dreaming for him.*

"Amazing, babe!" I said in my best play-it-cool voice. "I'm so happy for you. And yes, totally ask him to stay with us!" *Praise Jesus!*

sir, yes sir!

Ryan agreed to move in, and I began coaching him on how to code. In return he basically became the boss of my health—my workout routine, diet, sleep, water intake, all of it.

Slowly, I started to see a noticeable transformation in my body, which was rewarding. I was beginning to look like the old Dino my wife first met, the guy who used to run marathons. I had more energy and felt so good.

But the transformation wasn't just physical. It was mental and emotional, too. It felt as if a fog was lifting. I could feel myself becoming more mentally sharp, more patient, and—most important—happier.

The transformation in Dino affected his whole personality, and I was digging it.

"Babe, I mean this in the nicest way possible," I told him one night as he crashed into bed, "but since you started letting Ryan be the boss of you, you're so much more enjoyable to be around."

"I take that as a huge compliment," he said. "And look! I found my six-pack!" He patted his bare belly. "It was right here, under my blubber."

"Yeah, you're looking good, babe," I said. "I love seeing you so dedicated. I love how you're crushing these intentional goals you set for yourself."

"Well, your brother doesn't mess around," he said.

"But you're the one who's actually doing all the things," I said. "You're following through, working out every day, eating so well, and sticking with the program. Just saying. I'm impressed."

Ryan lived with us for about six months, long enough for me to develop a lasting rhythm of healthy living and for him to learn coding. By the time he took a job as a software engineer and moved out, his habits had become my own. I'll be forever grateful.

I really enjoyed the consistency of this new way of living. Each day, my body and brain knew exactly what to expect. The rhythm was almost addicting. It suited me.

I enjoyed being healthier physically, but it was more than that. I couldn't quite put my finger on it until one evening when Ash and I were invited over to some friends' house. After dinner, we gathered around their firepit, just catching up on life. I told them about Ryan's influence on my health and my habits.

"You look good, man," the husband said to me. "You'd grown a bit of a gut over the past couple years, no offense. But it's, like, gone. And you seem, I dunno, more chill. More content."

"That's exactly how I feel," I told him. "I'm shocked by how much I love this new rhythm of eating and working out. And being disciplined in one area of my life is starting to overflow into being disciplined in the rest."

And there it was. That's exactly what it was. Discipline was contagious. Gaining proficiency over one aspect of my life was rewarding. I now craved that same disciplined mastery over every area of my life. I was becoming more committed to completing the home projects I started. The kids could count on me to hang out and play with them every evening as promised. Even at work, I no longer procrastinated on projects I didn't enjoy. Instead, I'd jump on them and knock them out.

As they say, discipline is saying no to the things we want right now so that we can have the things we want most later. I had gotten a taste for what life could be like when I chose long-term priorities over living for the moment. I could see the man I wanted to become—the man God wanted me to be—and I was committed to sacrificing whatever it took to get there. There was no going back.

It felt like God had given me a little gift. I had watched Dino's body and health decline over the past several years, but I hadn't been praying that he would become as ripped as my bro. I wasn't looking for him to have a hot bod. Instead, I had prayed that God would help Dino grow every day; that he would seek after God, guide our family well, and have a desire for balance in his life. Most of all, I simply prayed that God would work in him.

I was starting to see how beautiful it was to pray for whatever God wanted to do inside my husband rather than for whatever I thought Dino needed. We had been through a lot in the first eight years of our marriage, and we felt good about the general direction of all things Petrone. I was learning that intentional design is essential—not only to transforming a house, but also to transforming our lives. I wanted to bring intentionality to whatever the next season held for our family.

finding contentment (even during a remodel)

In the first few years of our marriage, *budget* had become my favorite word. In this season, I fell in love with the word *intention*—as in, live with intention. Dino was modeling this character trait as he became a more disciplined man, and I wanted to follow suit in how I managed my own life.

Intentionality is a powerful word that applies to every aspect of our lives—our minds, words, bodies, diet, and time as well as our parenting, relationships, marriages, and homes.

I've found that deliberately choosing my thoughts, words, and actions changes everything, including my contentment with my home. Here are some tips I use to keep my satisfaction level high.

QUICK TIPS

▶ Speak your gratitude for the things you love about your home.

▶ Expect unexpected glitches—and plan for them.

▶ Overbudget the project by about 20 percent to allow for hidden expenses.

FINDING CONTENTMENT (EVEN DURING A REMODEL)

Contentment starts within, right? But we all need a little help when our space is driving us crazy. Here are some ways to remain content rather than frustrated when you think about your home:

>>> **Speak your gratitude.** Having learned what a difference positive thoughts and words made on my attitude toward my husband, I soon discovered that this kind of thinking improved my satisfaction with my home as well. Example: It used to drive me crazy that I couldn't remove the one weight-bearing wall that closed off my kitchen from the dining area. It became a constant source of irritation until one day, it struck me that while I couldn't change that wall, I could change how I thought about it. Instead of focusing on how much I didn't like my closed-off kitchen, I could refocus my thinking and say, "I love my open living room. How thankful I am to have space for my kids to run around." Soon I was regularly talking out loud to myself, praising the parts of my house I liked.

Walking around my house and reminding myself of the things I love helps me remain content. Speaking those words helps me focus on the positive. Give it a try! Find the things you love and speak your gratitude.

>>> **Expect the unexpected.** In the middle of a project or home renovation? Things rarely go as planned. We've had so many setbacks, I've lost track. One time, I had the genius idea to remove a wall that just seemed to be in our way. Dino and I grabbed our sledgehammers and started banging away at the drywall only to discover that the electrical wires for the entire room were within that wall. Oops!

Unforeseen setbacks like these suck—but they also stretch us. They teach us how to detect mold behind bathroom tile or how to move an immovable air duct. They improve our design skills, prepare us for future projects, and equip us with knowledge we can't get any other way. When you hit a glitch, focus on what you're learning, overcome the challenge, and move on.

>>> **Overbudget the project.** Partly because *budget* is my favorite word and partly because glitches always happen, I've learned that it pays to plan for projects to cost more than expected. In any home project, you'll end up making more runs to Home Depot than you can imagine. You'll find unexpected issues that cost actual money. Give yourself wiggle room. Overbudgeting (say, by 20 percent) eases the stress of those delightful surprises. Your project can stay on deadline because you've prepared for any hiccups that may arise.

PART II

simplify

06

less is more

I have learned to be content whatever the circumstances.

——THE APOSTLE PAUL, Philippians 4:11, NIV

On a beautiful Saturday in sunny California, Dino and I were up early walking, which was a part of our weekend routine. Our conversation centered on some exciting news Dino had received the day before. He'd been offered an engineering job at Netflix. The pay would double his salary, but the job would require us to move to Northern California. Also, the timing wasn't great for Dino's current company. He felt a strong loyalty to his boss and team, and accepting this new job would mean he'd have to break a commitment to them.

yes is yes

 I loved the job I had leading the tech department at the Hollywood firm. I had stopped working insane hours and finally achieved a healthy work/life balance. Even though I had made my family the priority over work, I was still young and wanted to continue to progress in my career.

I had applied for the Netflix job a few months back, along with a coworker who'd become a good friend. We had worked together every day for the previous eight years and had become a bit of a team. We promised each other that the Netflix jobs were an all-or-nothing deal: If we both made it, we would consider accepting; if we weren't both offered positions, we would stay put.

I was the weaker applicant. My friend is significantly smarter than me—like, by a long shot. Not even close. But after the interview process, I got an offer, and he didn't. We were shocked.

"Take the job!" my friend told me. "It's an incredible opportunity."

Should I uphold our "all or nothing" deal? The money made it really tempting to break it.

To add to the complexity of my decision, my company was being sold, and the sale required the current owners to hit certain profit milestones for the next year. I knew that it would be really hard for a new person in my role to hit those objectives. If I left, I'd be jeopardizing the sale of the company and hurting people who had taken care of me in my professional career.

On our walk that morning, it was hard not to see all the dollar signs floating around our heads. How I'd love to move to NorCal, buy a new house to renovate, and let my creativity go wild.

Dino's a verbal processor, and sometimes just discussing things out loud helps him find clarity, so I let him talk through all his thoughts about this decision.

"It sort of comes down to doing what seems best for our family—a big pay increase—and doing what's best for my team," he said.

I recalled a verse of Scripture I'd just recently come across during my quiet time with God. I thought it might apply to this situation.

"This morning I read from Jesus' Sermon on the Mount," I said. "One sentence really struck me. Maybe it applies to our situation."

"What was it?" he asked.

"'Let what you say be simply "Yes" or "No"; anything more than this comes from evil.'"[5]

The old me would probably have told him what to do or how to interpret that verse. Instead, I just shared what I had read and let him process it.

He stopped right there, halfway through our walk, and turned to me. "That's it," he said. "This is the clarity I needed. I'm not taking the job. It's not about work versus family. It's about character. I need to let my yes be yes and my no be no. I made a commitment to the company and to my friend. I'm keeping my word. Sound good, Ash?"

"Totally agree," I said, unaware that I did in fact agree until that very second. But he was right. It wasn't about money or opportunity. It was about whether to be a person of character, even when it was costly.

What may have looked like the wrong decision to other people was the right decision for Dino—and therefore, for our family. As much as I wanted a new fixer-upper, it felt right to stay where we were.

empty lot

We loved our Moorpark home, but once all the updates were done, I missed having a project to work on. For the past few months, I'd begun scanning nearby Redfin listings, a favorite pastime. True, we weren't moving to Northern California for the Netflix job, but I was on the lookout for a potential project nearby—a home that might provide a design challenge and would make sense for us as a family.

What caught my eye wasn't what I expected.

"Hey, babe, we're going out for dinner tonight," I told Dino. "I have it all planned. I'll drive. You just relax!"

He should have known something was up. I'd been conniving a plan all afternoon, ever since stumbling across a photo of a property for sale during my daily dose of Redfin house hunting. Building a home from scratch would certainly qualify as a new project! The design potential would be limited only by our imagination— oh, and our budget.

This listing was for a plot of land about five miles down the road, and at first glance, it had our names written all over it. There was plenty of space for our kids to explore, the commute to work for Dino was doable (always a major consideration in Southern California), and the view of the valley below and mountains beyond that was stunning. I imagined Dino and me enjoying our morning coffees from a porch overlooking all that natural beauty.

We hopped in the car to head to dinner. "Mind if I make a quick stop? I found a piece of property I'd like us to check out. It's on the way, so no harm. Okay?"

Dino gave me a side-eyed glance and grinned. "Fine," he said. "I should've known."

His good-natured response showed how much Dino and I had grown. He used to be the no guy and I was the nag in our home searches. Granted, today I was being a little sneaky with my "Mind if we stop by to see some land?" ploy, but he knew I'd been scanning Redfin for these past months, and this little surprise was all in good fun.

When we drove past the address in the listing, all we could see was a big old gully of land.

"Huh? That's it?" Dino asked.

We pulled over, and I opened the listing on my iPad. The property looked so different from the photos online, which showed an expansive view.

Turns out we were looking at the base of the land nearest the road, not the actual spot where a house would be built. Our eyes refocused upward toward the homesite, a glorious mountain of dirt boasting 360-degree views for miles.

We were sold. No begging or manipulating on my end. Dino and I both wanted this property.

We're pretty fast movers when it comes to decision making. No point dinking around. Dino called the Realtor on the way to dinner, and by the next day we were preapproved for a mortgage loan from the bank. We were going to build a home!

We'd need to sell our house first in order to buy that land,

and within a week, our house was on the market. It sold quickly, with a closing date sixty days later.

In just two months, we would move out of our very first home. Where does one live while building a house? I had no clue. Do we rent a house? Find an apartment?

Ideally, I wanted my kids to have space to run around, but the rental market was hot. Renting a home with a yard was out of the question. It was way too expensive in our area. We started looking at apartments, but even the rent on a one-bedroom apartment in Southern California was more than we'd been paying on the mortgage for our five-bedroom home. And a two-bedroom apartment ran about $3,000 to $4,000 per month, which would add up quickly. The contractor we'd hired estimated this would be about a six-month project, and we did the math. Yikes. No thank you! We needed to save money while we built, not spend more.

Renting nearby was clearly not going to work, so we started thinking outside the box. Lots of homes in Southern California have a tiny one- or two-bedroom guesthouse (called a granny flat or an ADU—accessory dwelling unit) in their backyards, which they rent out for added income. Maybe someone would rent us theirs.

That search didn't last long. Seems nobody wanted a family of five running around in their shared backyard.

We allowed our minds to run wild with crazy ideas. A friend of mine on Instagram brought up the idea of purchasing a tiny home to put on our property. I went to Dino with the idea, and he loved it. We both were all about it until we started looking at how much those tiny homes actually cost. Even a bare-bones model was beyond our budget. Back to the drawing board.

We were both sold on the idea of living on our land while we built. "What about an RV?" I asked Dino.

"Wow," he said. "It would be like the ultimate childhood experience for our kids—watching our home get built, being on an adventure together. And after the house is built, we could keep the RV and take road trips. I love it!"

Was this the perfect solution? We were not avid campers; in fact, neither of us had ever set foot in an RV before. But did that slow us down? Nope!

We went RV shopping that weekend at a used car lot in nearby Thousand Oaks.

Wandering the lot, we came across a 2003 Keystone Cougar camping trailer with a giant cougar painted on the outside. That animal was looking deep into my soul.

"He's saying, 'Buy me, Petrones!'" I whispered to Dino.

We stepped up the stairs into the Cougar. It was grimy, outdated, and cramped. Then we spotted three bunk beds—one for each kid—in the back. We looked at each other, eyes wide.

"It's a sign!" we said together.

Yeah, yeah. We've since learned this wasn't the only trailer in the world with triple bunk beds. Turns out it's pretty common in the RV world. But we were convinced this trailer was the one for us, so we paid $8,000 for a not-so-beautiful home, hitched it to our buddy Owen's truck, and hauled it to our new property.

cheers from instagram

It had been six months since I'd started my blog and begun posting to Instagram. At first, I just posted home decor tips and awesome deal-finds, and I was surprised as more people began taking notice. It was becoming clear that plenty of people also cared about making their houses feel like home. Soon I had seven thousand followers—which felt like a lot of people randomly following along with all my crazy ideas.

But once we moved into an RV, I'd no longer have a traditional home to do projects on. I'd be living in a tiny space. Would anyone still be interested in my posts? Would they care what I had to say?

Fear set in. I had worked so hard to build my social media presence. What if I lost everything I'd worked for over the previous six months? I really cared about my followers. I loved reading their comments and sharing their ideas along with my own. I didn't want to lose them.

With everything we had going on—only two months to make the trailer livable, pack up our house, and move—I didn't have time to worry or overthink. I just decided to let all my fears go. I remembered what my mentor Donna had told me when I first verbalized the idea of doing a blog: "Just be yourself."

Moving into a trailer with three kids—ages eight, seven, and four? Well, that was just me being me. That was us. Yeah, we're a little crazy. It might be messy. It might be a disaster, but we were doing it. Could I still be my authentic self? Absolutely.

I invited seven thousand online strangers to share in the journey.

180 square feet

I had a vision for this RV. I didn't want it to be just a camper we lived in for a few months; I wanted it to feel like our home.

Our new abode was a whopping 180 square feet of sand-encrusted blue carpeting, cramped built-in furniture, and nasty, outdated curtains. *Bring it on!* I was ready to start gutting. And I had just three weeks to complete the remodel before we closed on our old house.

Five of us were moving into this space, so I needed to make the most of every square inch. We ripped out all of the upper cabinets, the old sofa, table, and flooring. Fresh interior paint was a must.

I had a strong desire to live comfortably inside that RV. Once I'd stripped it down, I didn't want to overfill it with too much stuff. I figured we'd be there for many months while the new house went up, so I wanted plenty of free space where our family could thrive.

> *Moving into a trailer with three kids? That was just me being me. That was us. Yeah, we're a little crazy.*

"Let's make it bright and beautiful," I told Dino and then painted everything white. This made the whole space feel airy and open.

Instead of ripping out the entire kitchen, we refaced the cabinet doors. Many homes needing a kitchen makeover have cabinets that are in solid shape but have outdated doors. By replacing the doors but keeping the base cabinets, the kitchen gets an entirely new look, and it's a great money saver. Once the new doors were in, we painted the cabinets white, installed an IKEA butcher-block countertop, and added a cement-tile backsplash.

Because we wouldn't be moving the trailer around or traveling in it, I had a little more flexibility in the design. I did my best to stay within a budget by bringing in what I could from our previous house. By shopping at garage sales, IKEA, and Amazon for deals on furniture and buying only what we truly needed for the remodel, the entire renovation cost just $3,000. After paying $8,000 for the Cougar itself, we officially owned a newly remodeled home on wheels for only $11,000 out of pocket.

keep this, not that

Plenty of people hate relocating, and I get it. It's a lot of work. But for me, moving was way too much fun. We couldn't fit everything from our 2,800-square-foot house into the 180-square-foot RV, so we had to pare down our belongings—a lot.

My goal was to keep only what we truly needed for our new home on wheels, put the stuff we thought we could use in our to-be-built house into storage, and sell everything else.

I knew I was a chronic rearranger and organizer, but the process of sorting and minimizing gave me a high like no other. Oh dang, I love selling stuff so much! I had a blast.

I quickly realized how unsentimental I am when it comes to material goods.

I had zero desire to keep something just because of the memories attached to it. Memories didn't take up closet space, but things did! I figured I would keep the memories and get rid of the stuff.

Our house got emptier and emptier, until I'd whittled my own belongings down to one small pile in our living room. Same for Dino and each of the kids. Everything we wanted to keep for the future went into a storage unit we split with my parents.

The money we made from selling everything else covered the cost of remodeling the RV. With each sale of a piece of furniture or each trip to the thrift store with donations, I felt lighter inside. I felt good about this adventure. I felt free, as if all that stuff we'd owned had been tethering me down. I felt unshackled and pleasantly surprised.

The kids each had their own bunk bed in the trailer. We limited their clothes to whatever fit into a small plastic bin for each, which we planned to store at the foot of their bunks.

Pruning their toys was a little tougher. This trailer simply didn't have enough floor space to have a bunch of toys strewn about. My hope was that the kids would use their imaginations indoors and spend plenty of time outside exploring our property and just being kids.

In the end, I tried to make a game out of it. I handed each kid their very own shoebox-sized plastic bin and announced, "It's time to play, 'What can I fit in my box?'" They rose to the challenge and seemed to enjoy the process of deciding what

I felt good about this adventure. I felt free, as if all that stuff we'd owned had been tethering me down. I felt unshackled and pleasantly surprised.

to pack in their boxes. I loved hearing their conversations about what stuff they loved most versus what would give them the greatest possibilities when playing.

"I'm taking my Pokémon," Gavin announced, filling his bin with his collection of Pokémon cards.

"I'm taking LEGOs," said meticulous Gabe.

"I'm taking my sticker book and my favorite crafts," Quinn decided.

I also filled a bin with plenty of art and craft supplies. As with everything else, we helped them decide what to donate to the thrift store and what to put into storage.

To be honest, I was surprised by how well the kids went along with this plan. I'd expected lots of tears and complaining, but they actually didn't seem to mind that we were stripping down their belongings to the bare bones.

"It's an adventure!" Dino told them, and they went for it.

As I sold most of our belongings, I noticed something fascinating with the kids. Playing in our increasingly empty house, they seemed more content. Fewer squabbles. More fun. I wasn't the only one enjoying the breathing room. They were digging it too. Was I seeing glimpses of a positive change?

Our kids were so accustomed to relying on stuff to satisfy them, to entertain them, to make them feel loved. Dino and I were the same way. It's the American dream, right?

In this new season, I wanted all of us to strip away everything we knew and believed about our possessions—and live without all the stuff for a little bit. Would it be good for the kids? For us? What would we learn? How would it change us?

I began to look forward to this crazy new season.

simplifying your kids' stuff

Is it just me, or do kids' things multiply during the night? Every morning when I wake up, I swear there are more toys, socks, LEGOs, and books lying around. Even in the trailer, keeping the kids' few things under control was a constant challenge, but I was committed to staying on top of everything because we literally had no extra space.

It was more than just lack of space that motivated me. Helping kids keep their belongings under control teaches them important values. It encourages them to avoid consumerism and become good stewards of what they already own. Plus, it equips them to be tidy and organized as adults—and their future roommates and spouses will thank us.

QUICK TIPS

▶ Give your children choices about what to keep and what to give away.

▶ Let them profit from the sale of their things.
▶ Make it easy to maintain what they choose to keep.

SIMPLIFYING YOUR KIDS' STUFF

Here are three strategies that helped me get the kids on board with simplified living.

>>> **Give them choices.** Kids are more likely to get on board with simplifying (aka getting rid of) their stuff if they have a say in the matter. It's all in how you set it up. Begin by organizing their toys (or shirts or socks) into categories, then decide how many it's reasonable to keep. Let your child choose which ones stay and which ones go.

Let's say little Jennifer has twenty Barbies. Let her know she can keep her five favorites. Or if fifteen-year-old Jack has twenty-three T-shirts crammed in a drawer, ask which dozen he wants to keep. Setting a reasonable limit and allowing kids some say in the outcome give them a sense of responsibility. They have ownership because they're part of the process.

You can also let kids decide where to donate the stuff they're giving away after running through their options. Help them focus on the good they are doing rather than the loss they may feel.

>>> **Let them profit.** I mean, c'mon! Who doesn't love a fresh dollar bill in their pocket? Every few months, I'll encourage the kids to fill a bag with toys and goodies from their room. For each bag of gently used items, they get between one and five dollars (pick an amount that works best for your fam). If cash isn't a good motivator, choose a reward that will excite them—a movie night, new book, a mom date, etc. Invite older kids to help you with a yard sale, or help them sell items on Craigslist, Facebook Marketplace, or a similar site (with your supervision). Remind them that another family will be able to enjoy the stuff they donate. Decide ahead of time what to do with the earnings from items they sell—and then make sure it happens!

>>> **Make it easy to maintain.** "A place for everything, and everything in its place," as the saying goes. One of the biggest challenges for keeping a kid's room (or a pantry or your closet) tidy comes when there isn't room for the amount of stuff. Make

sure you've decluttered your child's room enough that he or she can quickly and easily put away everything you choose to keep. Fight the urge to add storage, since that goes against the whole point of simplifying. Instead, lose more stuff!

Once the available storage space equals or exceeds the amount of stuff, it's time to focus on upkeep. How can you create a system that is fun and easy for a child to maintain? Think baskets, bins, and drawer dividers. Keep everything easily accessible. For instance, resist the temptation to stack bins, because putting something away in a lower bin is a hassle, so it won't happen. Avoid extra steps for keeping the room tidy.

Next comes labeling, which helps kids (and grown-ups) remember what goes on which shelf or in which drawer. Use labels with icons for pre-readers and one-word labels for readers. This will make cleaning their room a breeze. It's like playing a match game. And it's so rewarding to open a drawer and discover that socks are in the sock section and undies are in the underwear section. Labeling also helps hold kids (and parents) accountable for keeping only what can actually fit into a space. Too many stuffed animals to fit in the basket set aside for them? Too many Hot Wheels for the car bin? If they don't all fit, something's got to go.

07

180 square feet

*Our life is frittered away by detail.... Simplicity, simplicity, simplicity! I say,
let your affairs be as two or three, and not a hundred or a thousand; instead
of a million count half a dozen, and keep your accounts on your thumb nail.*

—HENRY DAVID THOREAU, *Walden*

Moving day was pretty simple. We loaded our two cars with a few boxes of kitchen stuff, our bins of clothes and toiletries, the art-supply bin, and the kids' shoeboxes of toys. Once we drove over to the trailer, it didn't take long to unload and settle into our new space.

Dino had worked out a deal with our neighbor to provide the RV with water and electricity. We'd parked it near the boundary between our property and hers. For $500 a month, we were ready to go.

Disposing of sewage took a little more effort. An RV has two tanks—one for bathroom waste ("black water") and one for the water from the sinks and shower ("gray water"). Once a week, Dino and the boys would empty the two tanks into our neighbor's septic tank—black water first, then the gray water to rinse everything down. Not a fun job, but a necessity.

Did I mention we were now living in 180 square feet? Um, not sure if you know how big that is—or rather, how small—but it was a little shocking at first, let me tell ya. An average studio apartment is around 600 square feet, so we were living in a space about one-third of that. Think of an entire family of five living in the equivalent of a large bedroom. This was us, and believe me, learning to coexist in this tiny space took a little time.

Dino and I had a bedroom with a "fake" door in the front of the trailer. RVs really have no room for traditional doors that swing open and shut, so both our room and the kids' room had accordion-style doors that hung from the ceiling with three-inch gaps between the door and the floor. Super private for those romantic moments! And now that the contractor we'd hired was beginning to prepare the home site, we had excavators and dump trucks clanging around outside from dawn to dusk. The setting was practically straight out of a scene from *The Money Pit*.

The trailer had no dishwasher and no washer and dryer, which was a huge adjustment. But the bigger challenge was that we had no place to escape from one another. The kids weren't full-sized humans, but they were big enough to take up their fair share of physical space. At first, it felt like we were forever bumping into one another's arms and legs. Just moving past someone in the kitchen or living room (I use the word *room* loosely here) was a tight squeeze. We were snug.

Privacy was all but impossible. From the front end of the trailer to the back bedroom, everything was within earshot. Every word spoken, every door opened or closed could be heard by anyone else inside. This meant there was no hiding grown-up disagreements from our kids. Quarrels between Dino and me were awkward, to say the least.

less is more

About a month into our trailer life, Dino and I got into a fight over something stupid, as most of our disagreements were. The kids were playing outside, which gave us free rein to really let loose.

We started arguing in our bedroom. I can't remember if Dino said something to tick me off or if it was just me and my bad temper, but I got so mad I wanted to storm out of the room and make a dramatic exit.

I turned, scooted along the thin path between our bed and the wall, slid open our accordion door, stomped all the way to the other side of the trailer (a whopping fifteen feet), and stepped behind the kids' sliding door, "slamming" it shut.

I looked down. My feet were clearly visible through the three-inch gap below the door. So much for my dramatic exit.

Dino and I were quiet for a moment. The ridiculousness of this situation hit me hard and I tried not to giggle. All anger washed away.

"I can see your ankles," Dino said, stifling a chuckle of his own. We both busted up laughing. There was nowhere to go, nowhere to hide (literally) in our new home.

The sheer snugness of it all meant we were forced to work things out. We learned quickly that it was way more effective to talk through disagreements early and kindly before they blew up.

How I wish we'd learned to relate this way a decade earlier! It was humbling and eye-opening to both of us to see how unhealthy our patterns for fighting were. To be forced to work out every issue on the spot was real, y'all. There was no place to retreat or avoid each other when we were mad, so we were forced to communicate better.

We realized we'd spent years living somewhat parallel lives—and when disagreements happened, we often chose to pull away from each

> *As we learned to work out our differences in healthier ways, our connection became stronger and our commitment to our marriage grew.*

other rather than dealing with root issues. In our new tight quarters, retreating wasn't an option, so we learned to work out our differences in healthier ways. Our connection became stronger and our commitment to our marriage grew every day.

(D) I had turned down a dream job at Netflix, surrendered my childish hobbies and habits, and was investing myself heavily in things of value—marriage, family, and health. Ash and I had never been closer. She was true to her word about wanting to listen to me, stop nagging, and respect my opinions. I did my best to put her first in all my decisions and to listen to her with a yes mindset rather than my typical no. My walls of self-protection were coming down.

Trailer life was way more beautiful than I could have imagined. I loved every single second of it. Well, maybe not every second. Not showering in the tiny stall. Or emptying the sewage tanks. But still! Overall, it was a huge win. Without the trappings of too many material possessions, we had nothing to focus on but one another. I spent way more time playing and just talking with the kids. Ash and I became more flirtatious with each other and grew so much closer. I was discovering the freedom that comes from releasing my own desires and finding joy in the moment.

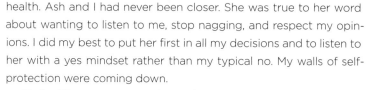

the greg challenge

We learned how to fight while living in the trailer, for sure. And the best part of reconciliation? Making up!

Intimacy was something we didn't want to surrender just because we lived in a tiny space with a three-inch gap beneath our bedroom door and three kids within earshot. Luckily for us, the kids got real good at playing outside—and all that fresh air and exercise meant they fell asleep fast.

Dino and I worked on being playful with each other, dating each other, and keeping things spicy between us. Thin walls and tight quarters weren't going to stop us.

One day Dino spent the morning video chatting with his three best friends from college. All of them were married with kiddos at home.

"I was telling the guys about trailer life," Dino told me afterward, "and Greg threw out a little challenge."

"Oh, really?" I said. He had my full attention.

A little backstory on Greg: I'd first met him when I visited Dino in his apartment when we started dating. From then on, Greg, Dino, and I were the Three Amigos. We hung out together all the time. We loved playing Mario Kart, and Greg and I would get way too competitive, but in the best kind of way. Years later, I still wanted to beat him at everything, and he felt the same way toward me.

"So what's Greg's challenge?" I asked.

"I was telling the guys about what it's like to live in such close quarters," Dino said, "and Greg goes, 'That's gotta be interesting for your love life.' I told him, 'Nah! We're holding our own.'"

I smirked at him.

"Okay, wait—it gets better. So then Greg says, 'Yeah, right. I bet you and Ash can't have sex for seven days in a row.'"

"What?" I said. "Challenge accepted, Greg!" I was in.

I'd like to thank Greg for that challenge. For the record, we whooped his butt—but in actuality, his challenge was a gift. Up until then, Dino and I thought our intimacy level was fine. We had sex maybe a couple of times a week, and we were affectionate with one another throughout each day. But we had so much fun during this weeklong challenge—not only with the physical intimacy but with the way it drew us closer emotionally—that we realized we wanted sex more regularly in our lives.

Dino felt so loved by all the affection and intimacy that he couldn't help but pour that love back into me. I noticed it in little things he did for me. It even affected how he treated the kids. I then felt so loved by his out-of-the-bedroom attention that I wanted to be more physically intimate with him. It created a loop that we wanted to continue.

Can I just say this might have been the best setup ever? Somehow I fell into a situation where my competitive wife was pumped about proving we could keep up our intimacy for a full week. Win-win all around!

I got a taste of a new level of intimacy with Ash, but I'd had no idea how much fun it could be and how close it would draw us together.

After just a couple of months in the trailer, I could already see how the decision to turn down the Netflix job had been the right thing. I was thankful that God had something better in mind for us. Rather than moving to a new house and earning more money, we were stripping away all outside distractions and discovering what our marriage could become.

I was doing my best to love Ash with the kind of love Jesus modeled—a selfless, sacrificial love that put others first. For a guy who'd spent thirty years riding the Dino train, it was quite a shift, but the more I put her needs before my own, the more she encouraged me and partnered with me as we guided our family.

This time in the trailer with no distractions reminded me of going on a meal fast—but instead of fasting from food, we were fasting from stuff. The stillness was clarifying. Once we were stripped of most of our material things, our true priorities became clear.

The lack of space in that trailer brought about a surprising shift in my life, well beyond my marriage. I had spent years clinging to material things and the fleeting joy they brought. I had always loved decorating, but in recent years, I'd begun comparing my home with the homes of others. Someone else's gorgeous house often made me feel less than, and soon I was in constant competition with those around me to keep up with their lifestyle. It was exhausting, frustrating, and unfulfilling.

Now I had no real option of keeping up. I had no nice home to invite others into. We lived in a trailer! Granted, we were hoping to build our dream home on this land. But this season of living in simplicity changed my perspective. I realized how very little a big house or expensive furnishings matter when it comes to finding joy and satisfaction in life. I was done playing that comparison game.

The lack of physical belongings also gave me back so much time. I had fewer rooms to tidy and less stuff to organize and maintain. I could clean the entire trailer top to bottom in thirty minutes or less. The lack of clutter also created mental space. I thought of all sorts of things I wanted to blog about, and I savored those quiet mornings at our tiny kitchen table, where I could put my thoughts into writing.

I also had more time to work on my photography so that my pictures could better capture this magical season of our lives. I began posting to Instagram more regularly. It felt great to be investing more time in my Instagram community—and this simpler way of life made it possible.

For the first time in my life, I felt free. For Dino and me, it was like shedding our old skins and leaving our former selves behind. He no longer had a home office, which meant we no longer had a gaming space. Everything that had once pulled our hearts away from each other and our family was gone. Our most important relationships finally took top billing in our lives.

As we sat together under the stars one night after the kids were asleep, I was struck by the sheer beauty of this moment. The view from our property took my breath away. The light breeze held the faint scent of pine trees, eucalyptus, and freshly dug earth. I had my husband beside me and our three kids asleep behind me in the trailer, tuckered out from a day of outdoor adventures on our property.

Dino turned to me, his face radiating. "This is just perfect, babe," he said, pulling me close. "I never could have guessed what this season would hold. Our time in this trailer is about more than just saving money on rent while we build a house," he said. "Something else, something bigger is happening. Do you feel it?"

"Absolutely," I said. "It feels like God drew us here for a reason. We've stripped ourselves of everything that once made us comfortable, and yet this is the most freeing, peaceful, rewarding season of our lives."

Dino reached for my hand. We sat there, silenced by the beauty of that night sky and filled with a contentment neither of us had ever known.

 I watched Ash transform during those first few months in the trailer. Her insecurities and tendency to compare herself to others just melted away. She even got rid of more stuff in our storage unit, realizing if we hadn't needed it for several months, we didn't need it at all.

I noticed a shift in who she spent time with as well. She no longer wanted to invest time in relationships that encouraged attitudes in herself that she didn't like. Instead, she began investing more time in her friendships with women whose lives seemed centered and content.

The peace this brought her was refreshing to witness. I loved and admired her more than ever, and I leaned into her. We didn't need more stuff. We didn't need more anything. We were enough.

We didn't need more stuff. We didn't need more anything. We were enough.

mastering minimalism

I've become a true believer in minimalism. People have different versions of what that word means, but to me it's not just physical; it's a state of mind. What gives you peace when you walk into your home? That's where I land.

Minimalism in the design world is often viewed as cold, stark, and uncozy. I felt the opposite about our trailer. We'd sold most of our possessions and were living with less. But that didn't mean our new home on wheels was austere and uninviting. I'd chosen carefully what to bring into our home. I'd selected color palates, textures, and floor coverings with intention. Being purposeful helped me create a tiny home that was rich with character. It was airy, bright, and cozy. Getting rid of the stuff we no longer needed, loved, or had room for was key.

In downsizing to our trailer, I became a bit of a pro at sorting our stuff. I still use these skills today.

QUICK TIPS

▶ Learn the art of sorting, deciding whether to toss, give away/sell, or keep each item.

▶ Let go of sentimental stuff.
▶ Follow the one-in, one-out rule.

LEARN THE ART OF SORTING

Maybe these ideas will help you feel less overwhelmed when it comes to deciding what to keep and what to give or throw away.

>>> **Start small.** No need to overwhelm yourself by taking on an entire room. Start by tackling one drawer, one closet, or even one shelf. Once you've mastered one small space, you'll realize how freeing it is to open that drawer or closet and find it clutter-free. Keep the ball rolling! Let that freedom drive you to do more.

>>> **Begin sorting.** As you clean out a space, place each item in one of three piles: toss, give/sell, or keep.

- **Toss:** If something is worn out or broken beyond repair, put it in the toss pile. And don't let your family rummage through it before you take it to the garbage can!
- **Give/sell:** If something is still in good condition but you no longer use or like it, donate it to a friend or charity, or sell it on Craigslist or a similar site.
- **Keep:** Only those things you truly use, love, and have space for go in the keep pile. To help your newly organized space stay tidy, label your shelves and choose containers for each type of item. Label the containers, too.

>>> **Keep on sorting.** Continue organizing and minimizing until you've worked through your entire home. But don't stop there. Develop an eye for spotting anything you don't use or love—and get rid of it. You'll be surprised by how energizing and freeing it is to live in an uncluttered space where everywhere you look, you see things you truly love.

LET GO OF SENTIMENTAL STUFF

I'm not the most sentimental person out there when it comes to what I own—and living in the trailer actually ramped up my unsentimental side even more. I sold my wedding dress for a big, old seventy-five dollars. Heartless? Maybe. But Dino didn't mind. That dress would have sat in a box for years—and most likely yellowed—until I finally sold it at a garage sale when I was sixty-five. Instead, another bride got to enjoy that beautiful dress at a bargain price, and I used the money for a night away with my husband. We created an incredible memory we'll never forget.

If I don't use something or love it, out it goes. I can better spend the time, money, and mental space it takes to maintain it. Maybe you're holding on to a few sentimental things that take up valuable breathing room in your life. Clutter has a way of doing that without our even realizing it. Maybe we can learn to let go of a few items we won't miss.

When trying to decide if you should get rid of something with sentimental value, ask yourself these clarifying questions. Your answers will help you release those items in favor of a less cluttered home and more peaceful life.

>>> **Ask Four Clarifying Questions:**

1. **Do I need it, love it, or have space for it?** If not, get rid of it.

2. **Does keeping it make me happy or stress me out?** If it adds stress, bye-bye.

3. **What's the real reason I'm holding on to it?** Guilt? Fear of hurting someone's feelings? Hassle to sell it? Resolve the real issue—and then let it go.

4. **Can I repurpose it?** Get creative and use the item in a new way that doesn't take up as much space.

Item >>>	Repurpose >>>
Grandma's sterling flatware or china set	Keep one serving spoon or make one teaspoon into jewelry. Keep one platter or serving bowl. Sell the rest.
Antique dresser	Use as a TV stand, baker's rack, or dry bar.
Kids' art, school papers, old photos	Scan and load onto a digital frame.
Antique vase or crock	Use as a planter or umbrella stand.
Memorabilia (china doll, signed baseball, old clarinet, etc.)	Put in a shadow box and hang on a wall.
Small items (silver baby cup, baby shoes, old photo, etc.)	Hang on the Christmas tree as ornaments.

>>> **Be intentional about where you donate.** As the saying goes, "It is more blessed to give than to receive."[6] Could an item you plan to give away be a real blessing to someone else? Do you know someone who might want it? By being intentional about where you donate your stuff, you can focus on the joy it will bring others or the good it will do, rather than the loss of letting it go.

I remember when I was helping the kids go through their stuff in preparation for moving into the trailer. Quinn had a giant stuffed bear she adored, but it was simply too big to bring with us.

"But Mama, Bear-Bear will be lonely if we put him in storage," she said, her big brown eyes filling with tears.

"Wow, you're right, Quinn," I said, pulling her and Bear-Bear onto my lap. "I wonder if one of your friends could give him a good home instead."

Quinn's brow furrowed. She was deep in thought. Then her face brightened. "Ezra could!" she said, referencing her friend from school. "He's my best friend, and he loves to hold Bear-Bear whenever he comes over for a playdate!"

And with that, Quinn put her bear in a bag and set him by the front door so we could take him to church next Sunday. She wrote Ezra a note and tucked it into the bag. Problem solved.

If no one you know wants the item in question, donate it to a charity. Rather than driving to the nearest thrift shop, find an organization that supports a cause you care about.

Where can you donate? Here are some possibilities:

- resale store that supports a local women's shelter
- refugee organization that provides household items or furniture to displaced families
- shelter for people who are homeless
- secondhand store that supports those affected by a medical condition (cancer, cerebral palsy, etc.)
- donation sites that accept building supplies for Habitat for Humanity

Knowing your contribution helped this cause will add to your joy and make it easier to let things go.

>>> **Follow the one-in, one-out rule.** Living in the trailer, I didn't have the luxury of bringing more stuff in because we simply didn't have the room. But I still loved a good deal-find. What to do? I created a little rule for myself that held me accountable and kept me from overfilling our space:

If something comes in, something similar must go out.

I still use this rule today because it forces me to really think about what I already own before I acquire something new. Do I want this new item so much that I'm willing to give up something else? If so, what would I let go of? If I don't want the new thing more than something I already have, then it has no place in my life.

The one-in, one-out rule might seem like a big mental step to take before simply buying a new shirt or wall hanging, but it makes a big difference. The end result of following it is that, over time, my home or wardrobe is filled with things I've been intentional about buying and really love.

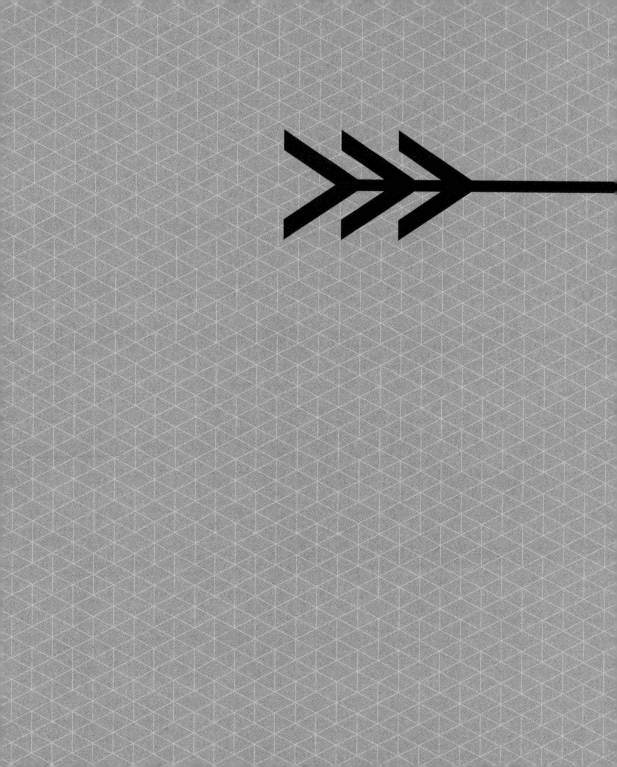

08

finding joy in the in-between

Once you learn to choose your belongings properly,
you will be left only with the amount that fits
perfectly in the space you currently own.

—MARIE KONDO, *The Life-Changing Magic of Tidying Up*

I immediately fell in love with the less-is-more concept after moving into the trailer. My grip was loosening on the things I thought we needed to be happy. I was being stretched to feel comfortable even when our house (aka trailer) wasn't perfect.

The contractor and his crew continued working on our homesite but our lot was hilly, which made it a complicated job. Quite a bit of excavation was needed before construction could even begin.

Our kids enjoyed watching the giant earthmoving machines brought in to do

the excavation. The sound of those powerful engines and the clang of their iron buckets hitting the side of our hill were no match for whatever soundproofing the thin walls of the trailer provided. Thankfully, the clatter outside soon became like white noise and we tuned it out, barely noticing it even when we found ourselves shouting to be heard above the racket.

Because we were living on a plot of dirt next to all this excavation, there was no escaping the endless dust and debris that followed us into the house. Our trailer was parked on a little space covered in mulch. Dino and I thought we were geniuses for choosing this spot. Less mud, less mess, right?

Wrong.

Mulch sticks to everything—socks, clothes, shoelaces. We tracked it into the trailer all day long. Poor Quinn, who had her father's curly hair, needed me to untangle the mulch from her head on a daily basis. Every night, each of us would find a nice little pile of mulch between the sheets at the foot of our beds. Super cozy.

life with kids, skunks, and bugs

Mulch can also be a breeding ground for bugs and rodents. *Lovely.* We once had a family of skunks camp out under our trailer for a week, digging for grubs. Stink bugs really loved our firepit area, and we discovered that if you squish them, they live up to their name. In case you're wondering. Trust me on this.

I'm not a fan of bugs. Never have been. My tolerance for insects was really put to the test when a swarm of Japanese beetles chose the tree next to our trailer as their love nest for a full month of mating season. My worst nightmare!

Most people would describe Japanese beetles as harmless—maybe even beautiful with their shiny green skin. They're not aggressive. In fact, they seem kind of dumb. They just fly around with no rhyme or reason. But every time I'd step foot outside, the Japanese beetles would spot me and fly straight into my hair. It became a running joke with the kids, who were unfazed by the beetles.

Me: *(peeking outside)* Kids, is the coast clear?

Gavin: Yep!

Gabe: Coast is clear!

Quinn: No beetles!

Me: Okay, I'm making a run for the car. Wish me luck.

I'd dash down the stairs and head for the car.

It never failed. As soon as I stepped outside, a half dozen beetles would magically appear, their loud, helicopter buzz right in my ear. I'd scream and flail my arms around my head and run as fast as I could, while the kids laughed their heads off at their crazy mama.

"Mom, it's just a bug," Quinn told me one day, patting my arm. "Don't be scared. That's nonsense." A four-year-old was telling me to buck up. Didn't help.

I knew it was foolish, but I didn't care. By the way, nothing has changed since. Every summer, I'm still terrified of those dang beetles.

Even with the bug fest, wandering skunks, weeds, and the mulch that constantly found its way between our sheets, the simplicity of trailer life gave me joy. I had been so intentional with the design of our tiny home on wheels that it truly felt like a refuge, a place where we could relax and get cozy. I had spent years trying to obtain this comfy feeling in past apartments and houses, but nothing had felt as peaceful as our trailer.

I realized I'd been going about it all the wrong way. I'd been filling spaces with countless mindless items I didn't love, which had caused me stress, created division in my marriage, and amplified the empty hole of an unfulfilled life. In the trailer, only my very favorite and most essential items had made the cut. Everywhere I looked, my eyes landed on something I loved and was grateful to have. It changed everything.

The boys were in elementary school, and Quinn was in preschool a few days a week. This gave me some sacred, peace-filled time alone in the RV when I could work on my blog, write, take photos for my Instagram, and tinker around the trailer.

> *In the trailer, only my very favorite and most essential items had made the cut. Everywhere I looked, my eyes landed on something I loved and was grateful to have. It changed everything.*

My fears that I'd lose my beloved Instagram and blog followers if we moved out of a traditional home proved unfounded. In fact, the opposite seemed to be true; people were fascinated by our RV lifestyle and the appeal of less-is-more living. I loved my @arrowsandbow readers and continued to learn way more from their comments and ideas than I ever dished out.

In those quiet mornings while everyone was at work or school, I found such simple pleasure in small things like taking walks in the woods or picking flowers on our prop-

erty. I was surprised by the big impact such little adventures made on my peace of mind and sense of well-being.

Those mornings gave me space to wrestle with big questions too. *What does the next season hold? What does it mean to be content? Could I design another home (even one on wheels) and use my talent without letting it consume me—without becoming competitive with the woman next door or a person on Instagram?*

I sensed that God was telling me I could. I'd spent a lifetime trying to soothe my sense of inadequacy with great deal-finds and the pursuit of the perfect home, but I was learning to tune out the noise of the world around me, rest in God's sweet peace, and embrace the gifts He had given me. I became more intentional about consistently checking in with myself on my motives, inviting God to reveal old patterns whenever they cropped up.

In this trailer, I was learning how seldom material things bring true happiness.

Whenever I felt tempted to try to impress others with my stuff, I'd stop myself and ask, *Am I doing this for me or for Suzy?* (I didn't know a real Suzy, actually, but "Suzy" became my go-to imaginary peer, someone I would be tempted to try to impress.)

To this day, I keep an eye out for Suzy. I challenge my motives, not only in home design or with my Instagram presence, but in parenting, marriage, and all areas of my life. This discipline keeps me on track.

D Ash's new habit of questioning her own motives before doing something helped me identify areas of pride in my own life, past and present.

I had really loved the big house we lived in before the trailer. I now realized it was primarily my pride that had loved the house. I loved having people over so they'd see how big it was—and how awesome I must be for owning it.

Then we moved into the trailer and my trophy house was gone.

I was really sad at first. All that space, all those bedrooms, all my things that I'd filled it with, gone. But as I let go of our old house and the unhealthy pride that held me captive, something else changed. I didn't just tolerate living in the trailer; I fell in love with it.

I'd come home from work to find the kids running around outside, thinking up their own adventures as they played on our land. I'd find Ash picking wildflowers and setting up the firepit for people to come over in the evening to hang out with us under the stars. This was in such stark contrast to our former lives, when afternoons were filled with television, iPads, and video games. Ash and I had expected more resistance from the kids about our shift away from technology, but they made the adjustment quickly.

We had nothing to our names except this tiny trailer, and wow, it felt so liberating. My tightly wound brain exhaled. I was free from the trappings of this world, free from worrying about a hefty mortgage, and free from the temptation to fill a house with all the things we "needed." It felt incredible.

We didn't have room for any big design updates in the RV, but I found joy in changing the tiniest things. I'd pick up a bouquet of flowers from Trader Joe's or cut some

greens from outside and add the simple arrangement to the kitchen table. The greenery and flowers added life to the room and made our whole home feel different.

A small shelf above our kitchen table provided just enough space for a few tiny decorative items. Whenever I was feeling a creative itch, I'd simply rearrange those items or swap them out with something new. The shelf and room would have a fresh, new feel. I was amazed by what a difference a little change-up could make. I fell in love with open shelving and with short, tiny glassware (because in RV life, ya know, the tinier the better).

Just a simple attention to decor filled my need to be creative. I started to see my creativity as a God-given outlet and beautiful gift rather than a curse that led to discontentment. By bringing in flowers or rearranging my little shelf, I was flexing a design muscle and growing in an area I sensed God wanted me to develop.

It was no longer about making a change (and then feeling guilty about wanting to make a change); it was about exercising my love of ambience, beauty, and a room that feels like home.

I was getting my wings and learning to fly.

I started to see my creativity as a God-given outlet and beautiful gift rather than a curse that led to discontentment.

trailer hospitality and the gift of dirty laundry

There was no shame in my tiny-house game. To increase our usable space, Dino added a patio just off the front door—not a real deck, just some outdoor rugs to keep the mulch from migrating indoors. We added twinkle lights and the firepit, and with the stars as our backdrop, it was our favorite place to be.

With a space to cook a meal and the firepit outside, why wouldn't we invite friends over and entertain? Dino started cooking and grilling a little more; I loved eating and entertaining, so having people over was a no-brainer.

I had lost all desire to use entertaining as a way to impress people. When friends visited, we focused on the relationships and how Dino and I could enjoy quality time with our guests, even from our little trailer.

Some people were into our RV experience and had no problem coming over. Others? I'm not going to lie. Not so much. For those friends, we brought the party to their house instead!

We had good reason to accept others' hospitality too. Weekdays in the trailer were filled with work, school, and the business of life. But when weekends rolled around, our family couldn't sit around to watch Sunday football or take a nap.

With five of us crammed into 180 square feet, napping was almost impossible. Anytime someone so much as sneezed, it felt like an earthquake. If we were stuck inside for too long, it began to feel claustrophobic, so we found ourselves wanting to either work on projects around the RV or load up the car and go explore.

Almost every Saturday, we'd take a little family adventure somewhere. Living in Southern California, the possibilities were endless. We'd always lived in places that had cool stuff to see, but until we were cooped up in a trailer, we'd never taken advantage of the amazing beaches, hiking trails, and activities within a day's drive.

But it wasn't all fun and games. Keeping up with our laundry required skilled planning. We had no washing machine or dryer in the trailer, so the weekends were also laundry days. Often, we'd just hit the laundromat, but whenever possible, we'd finagle our way over to a friend's house with a promise to bring dinner or babysit—and bring our laundry.

We weren't poor or unable to get to the laundromat, but we'd chosen to live in an RV without laundry facilities and didn't want to make our friends pay for our decision. Some of our friends really showed their love for us by opening up their homes during this season. Hence the offers to babysit and provide dinner in exchange for doing our laundry there.

Certain friends just knew we were hungry for community—for the ease of authentic conversation in the comfort of a normal home every once in a while. They welcomed us in with open arms, and I'll forever cherish their hospitality as the sweetest of gifts.

Prior to living in the trailer, Dino and I more or less kept to ourselves during our spare time. But tight quarters and the need for clean clothes forced us to leave our home on the weekends. To our surprise, we soon realized how much we loved it. It took dirty laundry to help us discover how much we actually enjoyed babysitting our friends' kids so they could go out on a date. What a simple way to bless another couple! We loved the rich conversations over dinner. These healthy relationships were super life-giving to us and remain a priority to this day.

experiences over stuff

Our monthly living expenses were few. Because we'd paid cash for the trailer and land, we had no mortgage. Besides paying for food and the $500 utility bill to our neighbor, we were saving money toward home construction. With no room for new gadgets and toys, what's a fam to do?

I'd made a deal with Dino before moving into the RV. "I want to allocate a certain amount of our monthly budget to having experiences together as a family every month," I'd said. "Think of it as a vacation budget but without the big trips. We can still put most of our savings toward house construction, but let's plan small, affordable adventures with the kids."

"Brilliant!" Dino agreed.

Wow, that was easy! The new Dino was quick to put us first, and Big Daddy was down for adventure. We settled on an amount to spend each month and set about planning.

Having something fun to look forward to at the end of each month was like a light at the end of the tunnel. We quickly realized we loved spending some of our discretionary money on making memories together.

One weekend, we decided to give camping a try. We drove to nearby Carpinteria Beach and chose a campsite near the ocean, where we pitched our tent. We waded in the surf, looked for shells, and roasted hot dogs over an open fire. We made s'mores as Dino pointed out constellations in the clear night sky. And all for about twenty bucks (cost of the campsite) plus a little gas. We came home with some good memories, but overall, we decided camping wasn't our thing. Living in our little trailer 24/7 was enough "roughing it" for our fam in this season. Lesson learned. But getting away from our routine—even on a short trip that didn't turn out to be our favorite—still had a renewing effect on each of us. We'd broken away from routine and done something out of the ordinary.

One of our bigger adventures was a trip to Mount Rushmore in South Dakota. Seeing the mammoth monolith carved into the granite face of the Black Hills was worth the trip, and I'll never forget some of our smaller adventures during that getaway. Once we pulled off the highway at a state park so the kids could stretch their legs. The park wasn't a tourist destination; it was just a local lake I'd never heard of. But the signs leading up to the exit showed it offered swimming, so we stopped.

As we pulled through the ranger's station and followed the signs to the lake, it felt like we were entering Tom Sawyer Island at Disneyland. The trees, trails, rustic buildings, and winding waterways were magical. We swam, hiked, and enjoyed the scenery until dusk fell and a horde of mosquitoes hurried us back to the car.

Unplanned discoveries like this were only possible because we made the commitment to leave our routine and seek out new experiences. Our commitment to adventure exposed us to natural beauty all across the United States. We learned our kids do well on these longer adventures. Road trips have become our jam.

That Mount Rushmore vacation was longer than our weekend trips, and it involved plane flights, hotels, and meals out, which were more than our monthly adventure budget. We had to save for it and use frequent-flier miles, but the memories we made were worth the cost.

I'm just not a very adventurous person by nature. If I have free time, I enjoy hanging out at home and resting. Before we moved into the RV, Ash was always asking me to do things together, go on adventures, join her in activities that interested her. Sometimes I'd say yes, mostly because I felt nagged into it.

But now I was committed to weeding out my selfishness and investing in something important to my wife, and she'd long ago stopped nagging. When she came to me as a partner with a plan for a budget change and some adventure, it was definitely a yes.

The kids were finding contentment and a sweet rhythm in the less-is-more concept too. They spent their free time playing on the hillside or in the giant excavation hole that sat just beyond our firepit. They had no other options but to lean into what was around them. I noticed them outside together more and more, using their imaginations to build forts, or hanging together inside, piled on Gabe's top bunk and coloring.

We had way less desire to shop. It's not like we didn't buy anything new, ever. But once we got a little taste of actually living life instead of filling it with stuff, the whole fam was on board.

Our commitment to adventure and experiences over gifts allowed for

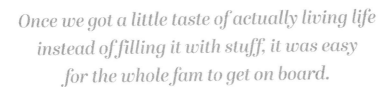

Once we got a little taste of actually living life instead of filling it with stuff, it was easy for the whole fam to get on board.

more trips to the zoo, more Friday-night runs to the ice cream shop, and more weekends away to focus and feed into our family unit.

Birthdays played out differently too. Instead of asking the kids, "What do you want for your birthday?" we rephrased the question: "What do you want *to do* for your birthday?" Same thing at Christmas. I'd purchase a few small gifts like books, a LEGO set, or an outdoor toy to unwrap on Christmas morning, but the rest of our holiday budget was spent once we answered the question "What are we gonna do?"

The kids made this adjustment pretty quickly, and family and friends soon got on board with our new less-is-more lifestyle. We had a great excuse: "Well, we just don't have room to store presents." Instead, I'd make a list for the grandparents of experiences they could do with the kids or that they could gift to them. If they felt the need to buy a physical gift, I was ready with a few ideas that would work well in our trailer.

Dino and I had fun with this kind of gift giving for ourselves as well. We got creative about learning what the other person loved to do—and then planning the next fun adventure we could go on together.

The longer this went on, the more I fell in love with giving experiences instead of gifts. Less was turning out to be way more than I ever could have imagined.

We were being given the gift of living with intention, rather than just cruising on by, dragging all our worldly possessions in our wake. We were learning to live life by design, with an intentionality that helped us make the most of every moment.

 Giving Experiences Instead of Stuff ⟸

Few of us need more things to fill our spaces. Instead of gifting tangible items to your spouse or kids, consider planning shared experiences with them. You'll create traditions and memories that will last—and those memories won't take up closet space when you get home.

Looking for a make-a-memory gift? Explore these search categories for ideas:

> **Interests:** Choose an activity related to whatever interests your family member or friend. Animal lover? Plan a trip to a farm. Water lover? Take a boat tour. Art lover? Visit a museum or arts fair.

> **Time-sensitive activities:** Look for events happening in your community, often listed on your city's online calendar. Theater productions, concerts, comedians, sporting events, and even movie releases are all great ideas for creating shared memories. If your budget is limited, check out free family programs hosted by your library, city or county, or local church. Many museums, zoos, aquariums, and local sports teams offer free (or heavily discounted) admission on certain days of the week or month. Check their websites and plan accordingly.

> **Lessons:** Take a class together to learn a new skill like making salsa, planting an herb garden, painting a picture, making candles, or brewing beer. Or share an ability you already have: Teach your loved one to make jam, build a fort, throw a football, or sew a quilt.

> **Year-round activities:** Explore local museums, zoos, or tourist attractions in your area.

> **Meals and treats:** Memories can be made over a cup of coffee or a sit-down meal. Plan coffee and pastries at a local coffee shop, or lunch at a favorite restaurant. Build an annual tradition of making memories together.

entertaining in the space you have

Do you avoid inviting friends over because you think your home is too small or not fancy enough—or because you don't have the right dishware or cooking skills to entertain? Don't let these fears keep you from making memories with friends in the space you have.

Whatever you have is enough because you are enough, I promise. Let's get over ourselves and our egos. Our presence is the biggest gift we can give friends because ultimately people just want to be together. We want to hang out. We long for community.

ENTERTAINING IN THE SPACE YOU HAVE

>>> **Focus on them, not you.** Home outdated? Too small? In the middle of a renovation? Remember that your guests are there to see you, not your house! Here are some creative ways to entertain in your space as it exists today:

- **Move the party outdoors.** Create a cool ambience in your backyard with a circle of chairs, a string of twinkle lights, soft music, and a hurricane candle. Bonus points for adding a portable firepit.
- **Go casual.** Don't have enough dishes or a big enough table? No problem. Choose a menu that works well on sturdy paper plates, like pizza, burgers, or brats. Then eat from TV trays—or from your laps.
- **Order takeout.** Remember, the focus of entertaining is on enjoying your guests, not wowing them with your culinary genius. If your

kitchen is under construction or you're unsure of your cooking skills, just order takeout from a favorite restaurant. Less stress on you—and a guaranteed good meal.

Instead of worrying about what others will think of you or your house, remember the point of the evening: your guests! By removing your insecurities from the equation, you can focus on answering the question "How can I bring joy to the people coming over tonight?"

Here are some great questions to consider as you plan a guest-focused event:

1. Does anyone have a food restriction or preference?
2. How can I help the kids have a fun night, while still allowing some meaningful grown-up conversation?

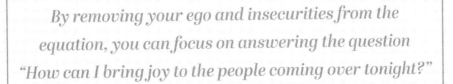

By removing your ego and insecurities from the equation, you can focus on answering the question "How can I bring joy to the people coming over tonight?"

3. Are they comfortable with me serving alcohol? If not, how can I make the beverage options feel special or celebratory?
4. Is there a birthday, anniversary, or accomplishment we can celebrate?
5. What questions can I ask each guest over dinner?
6. What's happening in their lives that they might want to talk about?

By thinking through these questions ahead of time, you can prepare for an evening that will make your guests feel loved and valued. Those worries of what others might think or whether your house is clean enough will fly out the window, and you can enjoy the true gift of their friendship.

>>> **Limit your cleaning.** *What?* That's right! Remember, the focus of entertaining is on your guests, and a person who enters an immaculately clean house is more likely to feel intimidated, uptight, or less than. While a gross bathroom or kitchen can be a turnoff, a little bit of clutter can help guests feel at home.

I allow myself only twenty or thirty minutes of nonstressful cleanup before friends come over. I give the bathroom a quick once-over, run a broom or vacuum over the floor, and put away clutter. I don't do a deep clean. While it's in my nature to tidy the house, I don't want to portray to others that our home is always

perfect. It's not. So I do my best and don't stress over the rest.

>>> **Include your kids.** Entertaining should be a fun family affair. I found that my kids, even at a young age, love helping Mama. It makes them feel important. When we have friends coming over, I give each kid a small job and then shower them with praise in front of our guests for contributing to our evening.

Depending upon their age and ability, kids can help with these types of jobs:

YOUNG HELPERS (PRESCHOOL AND ELEMENTARY-AGE KIDS, DEPENDING ON MATURITY)

- Pick up clutter and deliver it to the owner's bedroom
- Dust
- Sweep
- Cut flowers from the garden for a bouquet
- Clean the bathroom mirror and sink with glass cleaner
- Sweep the front porch
- Empty the dishwasher

OLDER HELPERS (PROBABLY TEENS, DEPENDING ON MATURITY)

- Light candles or build a fire in the fireplace
- Create a playlist of guests' favorite music
- Make the salad or dessert

>>> **Create ambience.** Flowers and candles cost very little but can transform the feel of a room. Grab a vase or even a large drinking glass, fill it with fresh greens from the store, your yard, or your neighbor's yard (with permission!), and place it on your table for a simple but beautiful centerpiece.

I'm a sucker for lighting a candle or two to add to the cozy element—and *boom* we're ready for guests!

09

the cost of change

Things change. And friends leave. And life doesn't stop for anybody.

——STEPHEN CHBOSKY, *The Perks of Being a Wallflower*

Moving dirt was becoming a way of life on our property. Every time our contractor finished one goal, it seemed another problem with the site would crop up. The preparations to build on our land were taking much longer than we'd been told.

With no real glimpse of home construction beginning, we were stuck in never-ending dirt work. Our short stint in the trailer would for sure be longer than six or eight months. We settled in for the long haul.

my instagram friends

Cha-cha-changes were happening. As I continued to share our journey on Instagram, I loved reading the comments my followers wrote—and many asked about the relational aspect of our family and my marriage. I couldn't help but notice that their interests had drifted beyond the physical aspects of our trailer, and they often had wise, insightful ideas to share with me—and one another. Among this growing community of home-design rookies like myself, God seemed to be doing so much more than just providing them with new ideas for the guest bath.

The Instagram group really began to grow. In the world of social media, I learned that how many followers someone has can grow exponentially. As my seven thousand pre-RV Instagram followers began to share our story, @arrowsandbow gained more recognition, and more people began to spread the word. Who would have seriously thought?

People seemed fascinated by our less-is-more story of selling it all. Travel magazines became interested in sharing our "designer" home on wheels via articles, blogs, and podcasts. And readers began engaging through their comments and ideas as they read about our family. It was astonishing to see the impact one little family's story could make just by being real about everyday life.

I think the rapid growth of my Instagram community is linked to people's desire not only to get great home-design tips, but also to see an authentic family with all their real-life struggles doing their best to love one another well and making some—shall we say—unique lifestyle choices.

"Just be yourself," my mentor had told me when I first started my blog. I'd been doing my best to deliver authenticity ever since. True, people wanted to be inspired with simple, doable ideas for their homes. But even more, they wanted to find relatable online friends with whom they could share their own struggles and occasional victories. That's why they were tuning in. It felt almost as if God was being sneaky, using this random home-design passion He'd given me to help people find my site—and once they did, many kept following because of our story.

The increased traffic was super exciting for sure. But was I simply doing this to impress my mythical "Suzy"?

I didn't think so. I was growing to love my @arrowsandbow community. Nevertheless, I needed to remain aware of my old insecurities and remember my "why" when it came to my new-found online friends. I needed to keep this about them. What would serve them well?

Change is hard. The change in our lives, both outward (living in an RV, having some success in my new career online) and inward (Dino's and my personal growth and maturity as a couple) didn't go over well with everyone in our lives. While our family and closest friends celebrated the direction our lives were taking, others didn't like it. In fact, Dino and I both experienced some losses in the friendship department. Some people simply ignored the good things we were doing with our lives.

A few were more direct with me. I was on the receiving end of a fair number of hurtful comments.

"Why do you spend so much time on social media?" one friend asked me over coffee. "You don't even know those people who follow you. I mean, your posts are cute, but home design? What purpose does that serve? Ashley, you know I love you, and no offense—but are you sure this isn't just about feeding your vanity?"

Ouch! I tried to keep tears from filling my eyes as I stammered out some sort of response. I thought of my imaginary "Suzy," and my commitment to analyzing my motives on each step of this journey. *Nope. My friend isn't correct. I feel joy in what I'm doing, and my followers feel joy in it too. We are becoming better people, not just better designers. And even though I've never met most of them, I feel I do know many of them—and they know me.*

As I drove home a little later, I realized this friend and I might have enjoyed our last Starbucks together. I didn't feel bitter, but I felt misunderstood and hurt. Her "Ashley, you know I love you, . . . but" said it all.

It was painful to be judged so unfairly, but for the first time ever, I refused to let someone else's words overpower the encouragement I received from most of my friends—and my growing certainty that God had placed me in this social media space for a reason. No way would I allow this criticism to change my mission.

A friend who knew what I was going through suggested I read the book *Uninvited: Living Loved When You Feel Less Than, Left Out, and Lonely* by bestselling author Lysa TerKeurst.[7] Well, the subtitle sure grabbed my attention! I figured, *What the heck? I'll order it and give it a glance.*

Best decision ever. I've since read that book every year, and I go back to it often for refreshers. It was like the author gave me permission to release friendships that were causing me harm. I felt released to let go of those relationships that sucked me into trying to fulfill other people's expectations and distracted me from God and my family.

Mind you, these friends didn't ask me to spend my energy meeting their expectations; I just took it upon myself to try to impress them and make them happy. With certain people, I was still trapped in the "What would Suzy think?" game. *Maybe if I just buy this designer bag, I'll fit in a little more or impress her a little more.* Or worse, *Maybe if I just agree with all her critical comments, she'll like me.*

It was exhausting, competitive, and unfulfilling.

So I stopped playing that game. I let go. I released the people in my life who actually made me feel less than. In their place, I began reaching out to girlfriends who accepted me and challenged me to become a better Ashley. That's where I

wanted to invest my time and my heart.

It was during our time in the trailer that I realized our homes aren't the only things that need an occasional makeover. Sometimes, sadly, we need to do a little relational downsizing to create space for peace and growth in our lives. It's painful, but necessary for growth.

I was becoming more confident and learning to see myself as God sees and loves me—as the creative, beautiful, thirty-year-old woman I was getting to know for the very first time.

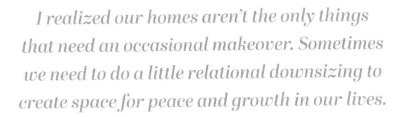

> *I realized our homes aren't the only things that need an occasional makeover. Sometimes we need to do a little relational downsizing to create space for peace and growth in our lives.*

becoming those friends

As in any relational fracture, there are two sides to the story. Dino and I reflected on our personal responsibilities in those friendships where we'd been hurt. What could we have done better? How could we have changed? Where were we at fault? What did we need to own and apologize for?

We tried to really lean into those questions and into each other, searching for growth, both as individuals and as a couple.

D I prayed daily that God would grow Ash and me closer together. Rarely does He answer our prayers by waving a magic wand and making it happen. Much more often, at least in our case, He puts us in situations that force us to grow—situations like this.

It was a painful time. We felt hurt and alone. Ashley wasn't the only one who had been on the receiving end of some harsh judgment. I'd also received hurtful comments from people I thought were my friends—people I thought knew me. My natural tendency when feeling attacked is to shut down and process the situation internally. For years I'd done this when I felt hurt by Ash, and I was tempted to do it now. But this time, I seized the opportunity to draw closer to my wife and work through it together.

We spent countless evenings sitting outside our trailer, talking about the pain of those broken friendships.

"I got your back, babe," she would remind me. "We have each other."

"Sames," I would reply. "Always."

Having a common "enemy" really brought us together. Our enemies weren't those people whose friendship we'd lost; the enemy was our pattern of self-isolating whenever we were put into difficult situations. This time, as some important friendships seemed to end, we learned to move toward each other rather than pull away.

One day I arrived home from work super upset.

"Ash, today one of our investments went way south, and we lost a bunch of our savings," I said. In our marriage, big-picture finances were my area of responsibility, and I felt sick with shame and guilt.

"Aw, babe," she said, wrapping her arms around me, "I'm so sorry. We are young—we don't need those funds just yet. I have faith in you. We'll be okay."

She said all the right words and I felt less ashamed, but I needed to verbally process this situation a little more, so I called a buddy of mine.

"Here's what happened," I said and then filled him in on the details of the sour investment.

He listened for a bit, but then cut me off, basically saying, "I also had bad things happen to me recently—and mine were worse. Let me tell you about it . . ."

Wow. It felt awful to have my loss compared to his and then minimized.

To our great relief, the bad investment flipped itself around a few weeks later, and what I thought was going to be a huge loss turned out all right. I called that same buddy to share the good news.

"Lucky you," he said, his voice dripping with sarcasm and self-pity. "Must be nice."

Again, wow. I wanted to be the kind of friend my buddies could count on. I'd just gotten a personal tutorial in what *not* to do.

That night around the firepit, I talked it through with Ash. "I turned to someone I thought would give me a little sympathy in my disappointments and then high-five me with my good news," I said. "In both cases, nope."

She listened, her eyes locked on mine, her face sympathetic. After a moment, she said, "Sounds like you know what kind of friend you want to become."

I sat there, mind blown. *Yes. That's exactly it. I want to become an understanding, sympathetic, and high-fiving kind of friend.*

Ash had quickly discerned what was really going on in my mind and heart, and I felt so safe with her that she knew she could cut right to the core. Rather than feeling defensive, I felt seen, known, and loved.

What she'd decided to leave unsaid was that I wasn't really the kind of friend who treated others with such care—not yet. I was often the one competing with a buddy over who had it worse when bad things happened or feeling jealous when good things happened to them.

I didn't want to stay that way. I wanted to become the kind of friend I'd needed these past couple of weeks.

"We've lost some friendships," Ash continued, "but wow, we've sure been given some great friends too. Great role models. They help us know what kind of friends we want to be."

We sat in the stillness, reflecting on the many beautiful ways our family and close friends had loved us so well in recent months. They had lent their washers and dryers, offered their homes for weekends away, and filled our hearts with memories made around our campfire, where the conversations had been rich and the laughter even richer. What great examples they'd set for us to follow.

"Okay, new Petrone challenge!" I said. "Let's promise each other that we are going to become better friends to those we love."

"Deal," Ash said.

"Let's crush it. Let's cry with those who need to grieve and take whatever time is needed to listen to those who just need a little support."

"And let's be our friends' biggest cheerleaders," Ash added. "If someone gets a promotion or has some good news, let's be the first people they call because they know we'll show up with dinner and a bottle of something bubbly, high-fiving them to the moon!"

Nothing fills Ash with as much joy as celebrating something or someone, especially if food can be involved. She was all in, eyes glistening, excited about our new plan.

How grateful I am for this woman. She's a gift from God. When I

Our marriage has become a well-oiled teeter-totter in the best of ways.

151

am low or need some wisdom, she lifts me up. When she's the one who's low or needs some insight, I try to do the same for her.

Our marriage has become a well-oiled teeter-totter in the best of ways.

coming in hot

About a year into living in the trailer, we were no closer to beginning the construction of our new home. The earthmoving was ongoing, and the conversations with our contractor were becoming strained.

Despite these frustrations, we were really happy in the RV. Our family was in a good rhythm. We weren't in a huge hurry to make changes.

Work was going really well for Dino. He was crushing every project put in front of him, while still sticking to realistic work hours and a nice family balance. His self-confidence seemed so solid—maybe a little too solid?—that when a recruiter at Netflix invited him to come in and chat about a job managing a software-engineering team, Dino didn't hesitate. He had turned down Netflix's last job offer because of his promise to help his old company through their transition. This time, he felt free to pursue a new opportunity.

 I was really happy at home, and I liked my current job. I didn't feel that pumped about making a change. But still—Netflix? Come on. If you're a coder like me, working for a big Silicon Valley tech company is the equivalent of playing pro ball. Running a team for a well-respected international company like Netflix? That was next level.

I told the recruiter we could have a conversation, but no promises.

I breezed through the first three phone interviews that week, and suddenly I was feeling pretty cocky. Things were moving along fast, which hooked my ego.

Even though this role was vastly different from the one they'd offered me seventeen months ago, I sort of figured, *Hey, they wanted me last time. Why would this be any different?* I breezed through the fourth interview. When they invited me to fly up to the Bay Area for face-to-face interviews and a chance to meet the team, Ash and I sat down to talk.

"I already dogged this company once by turning down their insanely generous offer," I said. "I can't do that to them a second time. And these first interviews have gone very well. If I fly up to interview for the job, there's no chance I won't get it. Are you gonna be okay with that?"

"Absolutely. I think you should keep going through the interview process," she said. "You'll fly up, crush the interviews, and get the job. Let's make some major life changes!"

It would be a twenty-four-hour trip. By the following night, I'd know if I got the job.

Because I'd been through the Netflix hiring process before, I knew what to expect. Halfway through the full day of on-site interviews, they'd narrow the field of final applicants. Over lunch, they'd let you know if you weren't cut out for the job. No sense wasting everyone's time. The remaining candidates would stay for afternoon interviews.

Morning interviews went well. In this role, I'd be leading a team of tech engineers, with the bulk of my time going toward leadership development and people management. I had managed teams bigger than this and felt I was more than capable of doing the job. I hadn't prepped for these interviews at all. Why would I? I felt unstoppable.

At lunch, they let me know I'd made the cut and would be moving on to the final phase of interviews. *Obviously.* I finished up the last few interviews, grabbed my bags, and headed to the airport, feeling great about the day, certain I'd get the offer.

My plane landed shortly after eight o'clock that evening. I was driving home when my phone rang. It was the hiring manager at Netflix.

"I'm sorry, Dino, but you are just not qualified, nor a good fit for the role," he said. "Here are the types of projects you would have needed experience with to make it through . . ." He then described several jobs and tasks on the human resource side of leading a team.

What? Don't they know I'm unstoppable as an engineer! Don't they realize every project I've ever touched has turned to gold?

I thanked the Netflix guy for the call and hung up.

I was devastated. Beyond devastated. This outcome had not even been a possibility in my overly confident mind. I had come in hot, certain I would lock this job.

I had already bragged to my friends and family that I was interviewing with

Netflix. "Yeah, they tried to hire me a year ago," I'd said. "Their offer was insane, but I turned them down . . ." *Ugh! How arrogant!*

My pride was completely destroyed. I felt so dumb and ashamed.

I got home and opened the trailer door. Ash saw my face and knew instantly.

"It's okay, babe," she said, hugging me. "It's okay. It doesn't matter. We didn't need that job. Life is good here. It's okay."

But oh wow, it wasn't okay. It did matter.

I lay awake late into the night replaying each interview, each question, each interaction with the team. And it didn't take me long to see what had happened.

I'd walked into the Netflix campus acting like I was the best thing that had ever happened to them—and they had smelled it. My arrogance had been obvious. They took one look at me, knew exactly what was going on in my overconfident head, and said to each other, "Yeah . . . no. No, thank you." And rightfully so.

I took the next few days to call each family member and friend to break the news of "Dino's Big Interview Day." I felt like a pathetic loser.

Those couple of days were good for me. I had time to think about how terrible my attitude had been, how prideful I had acted, and how quickly I'd reverted to an earlier version of myself. Where was my humility? What had happened to the Dino who wanted to put God and his family first? Where had that guy gone? How easily I had morphed back into the guy who wanted to be powerful and revered at work. *Ugh.*

From the first phone call with the recruiter, everything had happened so fast. I'd never stopped to pray about it. Ash and I had not sought the counsel of wise friends or family. I'd simply rushed ahead without asking God for guidance.

Once my initial shock and embarrassment began to fade, I thought about what the Netflix guy had told me over the phone—the types of experience I'd need to succeed in that people-management role.

"But I've managed a team before," I told Ash one night after the kids were in bed. "It's not like I had no experience."

"Yeah, but you hated it," she reminded me. "You hated managing people. It was time-consuming and messy."

She nailed it. My brain is wired to solve problems, but people problems are not the same as coding problems. My strengths are in creating software solutions to help teams thrive, not in managing people.

"You're so right," I said. It was beginning to dawn on me that I might have dodged a bullet. "This job might have cost me my hard-earned work/life balance and my sanity."

When I think back on that job rejection it still stings a bit, but it humbled me in the best of ways. More importantly, it clarified what I'm good at—and what I'm not.

Six months later I got another call from Netflix. They wanted me to interview for the original role—the one I'd turned down almost two years before. This job was indeed a fit for my strengths as a software engineer.

But what about our dream of living in a home we built on this land? Ash and I talked about it at length.

"We haven't even begun construction on the house," Ash said. "We're still moving dirt around."

"Yeah, I know," I said. "It sucks. But I don't think we should approach this decision with that as our only filter. Every time we face a big decision by starting with the practical side, we end up forcing things. We've been praying off and on about a potential job change for months, and I sense this might be the path God has for us. Let's dream a little. What could a move north look like for our family?"

"Well, every time I daydream about it, I can see it so clearly—just the five of us, off on a new adventure. A new house to remodel, new friends we haven't even met yet, and a new job challenge for you."

"Totally! I can so see it happening. It's like God painted a picture in my mind, and I love it, even though it looks completely different from the current picture we're painting, from where we thought we were heading. Would you be okay moving farther away from your family—and leaving this 'build a house' dream behind?"

"Yep. I'll miss my family like crazy, but it's still drivable," Ash said. "Plus I'm just in a much better place than I was at twenty when we moved to Vegas. And I'm actually getting pumped about the idea of finding a new house to remodel."

"So we both feel at peace about a move?"

"Excited, even!"

"Okay! On the practical side, we do need to sell the land, but I've been running numbers all morning. If the salary and package they offered last time is any indication, we're good." I looked at Ash. Her eyes were shining.

"Time for a change, babe," she said.

"Time."

We then sought input from trusted friends. I prayed, asking God for wisdom on how to best approach the interviews—and I studied my butt off. Getting shut down last time was still fresh in my mind, and I'd been humbled. No way was I coming in hot for these interviews. I wasn't going to make the same mistake twice.

The meetings went well. The job was a fit. A week later, they made an offer. We listed our piece of land for sale, and just like that, we were moving to the Bay Area.

Our time living in a trailer was coming to an end. It had passed in the blink of an eye. Our dream house had never been built. We'd spent all our construction money moving dirt, but I wouldn't trade those days for anything.

It had been the best seventeen months of our lives. We'd watched our kids grow closer than ever. They had become one another's best friends. And Dino and I truly found joy in our marriage, in our lives, and in our family and close friends.

We'd wanted to build a giant house where we could raise our kids and grow old together. Instead, we got so much more. We'd made simplicity our way of life. With almost nothing to our names, we'd discovered we really didn't need stuff to make us happy. Inside the walls of 180 square feet, we were enough. We'd learned what it means to truly live, to count the cost of change—and to find joy in the in-between.

relational rightsizing

Whether living in a 180-square-foot trailer or a five-bedroom house, I had come to realize that unhealthy relationships sap my peace and joy faster than tacky wallpaper or outdated furniture. Creating a peaceful home is about more than minimizing and remodeling. It's about being good stewards of our relational worlds, too, and making sure every relationship is one we need, love, and have room for.

▶ Clear the clutter of
unhelpful relationships.
▶ Become the kind of friend
you wish you had.

▶ Grieve with those who
grieve.
▶ Celebrate with those who
are happy.

RELATIONAL RIGHTSIZING

≫ **Clear the clutter of unhelpful relationships.** Relational downsizing is a real thing, y'all. Sometimes we're spread too thin by trying to cram too many relationships into our lives. Sometimes we just need to release those friendships that are toxic or unhealthy. I like to check in with myself regularly to ask myself these questions:

- **Does this friend challenge me to grow?** In other words, can I count on this person to be a truth teller? Or does this friendship actually leave me feeling worse about myself? Does this person's input into my life encourage me with healthy conviction or defeat me with toxic judgment?

  True friends sometimes tell us hard things because they love us. They want us to grow, and they're willing to speak truth to help us make that happen—and they do so with kindness. Unhealthy friends criticize to tear us down or make themselves feel better. Those are friendships we can do without.

- **Is this friend too much of a people pleaser?** Do I call this person because I know they will always agree with me, even when I'm wrong? I mean, who doesn't

love a good ego boost? Who doesn't love always hearing they're right? This kind of friendship is tempting because it strokes our ego, but I try to steer clear. These aren't people I can call when I'm looking to grow—personally, relationally, or spiritually. I need people in my life who love me enough to tell me when they think I'm wrong—and who can do it in such a way that I feel valued rather than hurt.

- **Am I just trying to avoid dealing with conflict?** I don't want to use relational downsizing as an excuse to avoid dealing with disagreement. If there is an issue between me and another person, I seek to resolve it rather than walking away from the friendship. Once I've done everything in my power to fix the problem, then I can evaluate whether this is a friendship I want to maintain.

- **Do I value this friendship primarily because it's an ego boost?** Do I maintain this friendship because the person is influential or "popular" in my circle, even though we don't have much in common? Am I tempted to name-drop to boost my own ego? If I'm only friends for appearance's sake, this is a relationship I should let go of. I'm using that person rather than valuing them as an individual.

- **Am I staying in this relationship because of "but they need me" guilt?** Certain people attract friends through ongoing personal drama. They constantly need to be rescued. Sometimes I get sucked into those relationships without realizing that it's not helping either one of us. While it's good to help a friend in need, it's not good to stay in a relationship out of pity or to become codependent with someone whose life needs more help than I can provide.

- **Is the season of this friendship drawing to a close?** Sometimes a friendship has run its course and

it's time to turn a page in my life. It's no reflection on the other person; it's just a shift in seasons. This doesn't mean I stop speaking to the person or never grab an occasional coffee with her to catch up. But I may want to invest fewer of my relational hours in that friendship and more hours with others.

There is no reason for guilt in letting go of friendships that no longer build value into our lives. Our time and emotional well-being are worth protecting and stewarding well.

Pray about the relationships in question and ask God to help you navigate through those waters. God wants us to seek reconciliation, peace, and unity, but sometimes that's just not an option. Sometimes

Relational Rightsizing

Are you holding on to a friendship that is no longer life-giving? The following questions can help you decide whether you need to make changes to your friend list:

> Does this friend challenge me to grow?

> Is this friend a people pleaser or a loving truth teller?

> Do I want out of this relationship just to avoid dealing with a conflict?

> Am I maintaining this friendship because it's an ego boost?

> Am I staying in this relationship out of guilt?

> Is this friendship's season drawing to a close?

we find ourselves stuck in friend-ships that are getting in the way of what God has in store for our lives. Be open to weeding out unhelp-ful relationships so you can create space for the friendships that will add true value to your life.

>>> **Become the kind of friend you wish you had.** After his buddy failed to show up for Dino the way he had hoped, we challenged ourselves to become the kind of friend we both want to have. I thought back to the days before my miscarriage and how little I understood about that kind of loss. No doubt I had friends who had miscarried back then, and I hadn't really shown up for them in the way they deserved. Now having experienced the depth of that pain, Dino and I were better equipped and motivated to grieve with others in their losses.

The same is true when it comes to celebrating. When we announced Dino's new Netflix job to our family and inner circle of friends, they cheered for us with their whole hearts. They set aside their own sorrow over our move hundreds of miles away and focused on celebrating with us. We knew firsthand how great it was to feel support and happiness from those you love—and we wanted to celebrate others' good fortune with them moving forward.

Here are some specific things we've found helpful when it comes to showing up for our friends:

GRIEVE WITH THOSE WHO GRIEVE

- **Don't pretend nothing hap-pened.** Your friend's grief is front and center in their minds, so just ask them how they're doing. If it feels uncomfortable, it's okay to say, "I feel awkward but I just want to check in on you." Invite them to talk about their loved one and their loss if they feel like it, or just sit and cry with them if that's what they want.

- **Use the name of the loved one who has passed.** As years go by, that loved one's name becomes like music to our friend's ears.

- **If they've lost a job, pet, or home, or if they've gotten divorced, much of this still applies.** Ask how they're doing. Do your best to be a safe space for them to talk about what they're going through.

- **In any type of loss, give practical help.** Don't extend vague pleasant-ries like "If you need anything, just call." Instead, make more pushy offers like "We'd like to bring you dinner next week. Does Friday work? Do you have any food pref-erences?" Or "Let me drive your kids to soccer practice for the rest of the month." Or even "I'm coming over to clean your bathrooms. See you in an hour." Put your love into action.

- **Add alerts to your calendar so you can remember those hard milestones—first Christmas, first birthday, first anniversary after a loss.** Reach out and check in on those hard days. Send a card or just shoot them a text to say, "Thinking about you today. Praying for you."

CELEBRATE WITH THOSE WHO ARE HAPPY

Whether it's good news or a cool accomplishment, here's how we love to celebrate our friends.

- **Be spontaneous!** Show up on their doorstep with a bottle of champagne (or sparkling cider, if that's your jam) and an ice-cream cake.

- **Offer to host a party** to celebrate the occasion. Or offer to cook and then clean up after the party if they want to host it at their house.

- **Celebrate them on social media—** but ask permission first. They may not want the world to know they're turning forty or just accepted a new job—before they've told their current boss!

- **Say it like you mean it.** When you see them in person, make eye contact and tell them specifically what you love about them or why you're celebrating them. Words of affirmation go a long way toward making someone feel truly loved and valued.

Whether you're gathering to celebrate with friends or to grieve with them, show up with food. It makes everything a little bit better, am I right?

PART III

soar

10

1,300 square feet

Every new beginning comes from some other beginning's end.

—SENECA, ancient Roman philosopher

"Bye, house!"

We all yelled and waved as the sweet new owners drove away with our little home on wheels. After we'd posted the trailer for sale on my Instagram, it had sold quickly—and at a profit. The couple who bought it were planning to live in it with their kids to save money. We clicked with them right away, and it was a bittersweet moment as they drove off.

While we were excited to begin a new adventure in the Bay Area, we had grown to love being stretched emotionally and spiritually while crammed together physically for the last year and a half in that RV.

And just like that, we were on our way north. We loaded a small U-Haul with our few items from the trailer. Seven bins, a few mattresses, and a couple other household items were all we pulled behind us as we drove north.

Dino's new job at Netflix came with corporate housing for the first three months, which gave us the flexibility to go slow and take our time looking for a new home to buy. But "taking our time" is not how Dino and I work. Slow? Ha! We don't know that word. As soon as I heard Dino say, "I got the job up north!" I had begun looking for properties on my Redfin app.

"On it, babe!" I told him. I loved hunting for a house we could turn into a home.

so much space!

The area we were moving to was filled with 1930s homes that had lots of charm. Most of the homes were less than 1,500 square feet with two or three bedrooms and one bath—which, after having lived in a mere 180 square feet for seventeen months, sounded gigantic. The fact that we would have a bedroom and a bathroom with real doors as well as our own washer and dryer—I mean, we felt like royalty.

When picturing our next home, I had envisioned a storybook cottage-style house or one with some European flair that I could bring back to life. But three days into living up north and searching Redfin, I found a house in our price range that had room for a family of five and a spacious backyard—a rarity in the Bay Area. It was a 1,300-square-foot Spanish bungalow with three bedrooms, one bath, and a little granny flat[8] in back. Five days after moving, we signed the paperwork and bought the house.

And the moment we signed, buyer's remorse set in.

"Spanish bungalow? What did we just do, babe?" I asked Dino. "I didn't want a Spanish-style house. I was hoping for Victorian or Craftsman or even Tudor. I know nothing about Spanish. Why did we settle on this?"

"This is an opportunity for you, Ash," he said. "What a great challenge! Maybe you don't know anything about Spanish design yet, but you'll learn, and you'll crush it."

It was just the pep talk I needed to hear. My wheels started spinning, and I was ready to dominate our next home-remodel project. As added incentive, the kids were definitely ready to begin our new lives inside their new home. Apartment life—even on Netflix's nickel—wasn't our favorite.

The house was in livable condition, but we wanted to make a few changes before moving in to make it our own. We had a month before the closing date, but the house was already vacant, so I had plenty of time to get everything lined up for the remodel.

First order of business: Remove the wall between the kitchen and dining room. Because you know I hate walls. This is something I've done in almost every home we've owned. I walk in and immediately begin searching for walls that keep the home feeling boxy and closed off. *Are you a non-weight-bearing wall that cuts off space unnecessarily? Bye-bye.* Our Spanish bungalow had such a wall. It kept the kitchen isolated and made the living room feel small. Goodbye, wall.

My remaining plans for the remodel were simply to paint the interior and refinish the floors—a last-minute decision, but oh man, one of the best! Seeing

those original hardwoods brought back to life completely changed the look of the house and made it feel brand-new.

Move-in day was quick and easy since we had so few things to unload. That first night in the new house, we ordered pizza and ate it on the family room floor—the start of a new moving-day tradition.

Once we moved in, I took my time honing my stenciling skills to add personality to our new home. I pulled out an old text message Dino had sent me and stenciled its words on the wooden stairs to his basement hangout: "I'm just blown away that you are mine!" I painted the old wooden fence in our backyard white, then stenciled geometric patterns in black over the white to give it some pop.

My mom even helped me do something similar with the front patio, where the original Spanish tiles were cracked and slanted but replacing them was out of our price range. We applied cream and terra-cotta outdoor paint to make them look like Spanish mosaic tiles—at a fraction of the cost.

I fell so in love with stenciling that I began looking for opportunities to use my new skills. I painted our front step with tiny hexagon-tile shapes in black, leaving some of them white to create the word *hello* in chunky cursive. Too much fun! Dino was right—this house was stretching me as a designer.

I took my time when it came to finding furniture for our bungalow. I didn't want to lose the lessons on minimalism we had learned in the trailer simply because we now had a little more space (okay, a lot more space!). I searched online and scoured Craigslist and Facebook Marketplace for one-of-a-kind pieces and hit up my favorite discount stores for amazing deal-finds. If the price didn't make sense or if I didn't absolutely love the item, I waited. I was intentional about not adding a bunch of stuff just to fill space.

I was captivated by the dream of a home filled only with things we actually loved. It was fun sharing that process on my Instagram account as well.

It's easy to get stuck in the race of doing what you see everyone else doing on social media or trying to create a perfectly styled home just so you can post a photo or feel like you're keeping up. But I had run that race before and learned my lesson. My imaginary friend, Suzy, and I were done with the comparison game. I was happy to stay as far from that temptation as possible.

On Instagram, I shared the process of filling our home slowly, piece by piece, and waiting for exactly what I wanted. My community followed along, and we all cheered together whenever I found a hidden treasure. Yeah, the intentional, slow route left empty gaps on my walls and some spaces that just didn't get filled. But actually thinking through each purchase was a mindful, peaceful process. And it was oh-so-satisfying when I finally hit the jackpot and found the perfect piece.

What I didn't take my time on was the guesthouse in the back. Our family of five had moved away from everything and everyone we knew. We wanted visitors! I worked immediately on getting that space refinished and filled with furniture for any guests who wanted to stay with us.

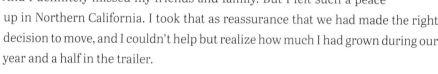

I was afraid that once all the excitement of moving had worn off, I would start to feel lonely or sad about being so far from family. This was a much longer drive than Vegas had been. But that feeling never came. It wasn't like me not to feel empty or like I was missing out on something. And I definitely missed my friends and family. But I felt such a peace up in Northern California. I took that as reassurance that we had made the right decision to move, and I couldn't help but realize how much I had grown during our year and a half in the trailer.

Moving up to the Bay Area was incredibly exciting. A new job, a new home, no more dumping poop tanks every weekend—wow, was I spoiled. Those first few months were crazy. I was learning my job (one where I was expected to perform at a high level), we were renovating the house, and we were helping our kids adjust to their new lives in the Bay Area. It was a crazy time, but we had learned an amazing lesson while living in the trailer: lean into the chaos, don't recoil from it.

Buying that little house scared me, however. I was terrified of going back to what we had been. The trailer had forced us into a season of fasting from things. Would our prior obsessions come flooding back? Ash and I talked at night about not wanting to lose ourselves now that we were once again living in a traditional house. We loved who we had become: adventurous, minimalist people who found joy not in our possessions, but in each other.

The clarity that trailer life brought was incredibly refreshing, and neither Ash nor I wanted to spend one more second trapped by our old overfilled way of living. When you spend time without the things you think bring you comfort, you find comfort in the things that really count. What mattered to me was us. I was no longer obsessed about the house we lived in, the job (or job title) I had, or the amount of money we were making. Living in that trailer helped me replace those concerns with priorities that brought true fulfillment: my relationship with God, my wife, and my family.

My reflexive fear had me expecting the worst each day when I came home. I subconsciously assumed Ash would fall into her old shopping habits and fill the house with stuff as quickly as possible. But it never happened. Each item Ash brought home looked like a treasure she had found, not just something she'd bought to fill a space. Her intentionality and discipline were impressive. I soon realized how little she cared about what others thought. She was no longer tempted to fall prey to house gluttony.

Things were so very different from the last time we'd lived in a traditional house. In that five-bedroom home, Ash was constantly purchasing, changing, and updating. This was not like that. She was completely happy living with the house empty because she wanted to make this house feel special, like an extension of our family. She wanted every last detail to be intentional.

And it was. That house was incredible. It had a feel that was just *different*. People commented on it. It didn't feel like we had filled the space; it felt like each item Ash added to the house was contributing to the very soul of our home.

> *When you spend time without the things that bring you comfort, you find comfort in the things that really count.*

"Let's get crazy, babe," I said to Dino about six months into our new home.

"Okaaay. What now?" He eyed me suspiciously.

"Hear me out. What if we turned our guesthouse into an Airbnb?"

We had already spruced up that space. It was the perfect little spot for guests, and I was hungry to expand my knowledge of hospitality and design to the next level. I envisioned it like this: A cute little Spanish *casita* stood waiting for guests to arrive. Our family and friends had first dibs, of course, and I'd personally clean and add my design touch each time anyone came to stay—a vase full of fresh flowers, a few beverages and snacks in the kitchen, and maybe even a mint on the pillow. (Clearly, I've watched way too many shows on this . . . LOL!)

Dino was on board with my crazy idea. Woohoo!

I immediately researched the area to see what others were doing. I read a bunch of articles and blogs on how to run a safe and successful Airbnb, and a month later, we were open for business.

It was a sweet little side business that kept my creative juices flowing, and the extra income didn't hurt either. We met the most wonderful people and even made new friends through that little backyard retreat.

I mentioned our own Spanish bungalow was tiny—I mean it was big for us after the trailer, but on the smaller size for a family of five. I called it the hobbit house because it had several interior archways that were so low, our taller friends had to duck when they passed through. But it was *our* hobbit house, and it was so cozy.

After living there for a year, we began to crave a tiny bit more privacy. The house had only one bathroom. I mean, we love our kids, but man—the pee on the bathroom seat, toothpaste on the counter, and towels on the floor were just about enough to drive us mad. There had to be a solution.

A small hobbit hallway off the living room led to the existing bathroom and all three of the bedrooms. At the entrance to that hallway was a walk-in coat closet that held nothing but our vacuum and a few coats. It seemed like the perfect spot for a second bathroom.

"Let's rip out another wall!" I told Dino over dinner one night. "And by wall, I mean let's blow a hole through the hallway closet and expand it into Quinn's bedroom closet. It would make her room a little bit smaller, but we could turn that new space into a bathroom for the kids!"

All Dino needed to hear was "a bathroom for the kids," and he was sold.

Why not utilize every space in the house for function? Because we didn't have a bunch of extra stuff to store in that closet, we had the flexibility to do something more practical with that space. We didn't need a second bathroom to survive, but it would make each morning more enjoyable for all of us. We decided to break from the norm, ditch the traditional closet, and do what worked best for our family of five. We added another bathroom because we wanted to, because we had the vision to, and because we wanted to thrive in this home.

Running a successful Airbnb in our backyard? Check! Converting hallway closet to second bathroom? Check! Stencil every surface I could think of? Check! Now what? Where did we go from here?

Dino was happy and loving his new job. His commitment to maintaining a healthy work/life balance was a gift to our family. We had been living in this cute house for about fifteen months, and I'd done all the fun things to it I could think of. Now we were kind of at a standstill with projects. With everything done, we began to feel restless. I wasn't in the business of redoing things just for the sake of redoing them, but Dino and I loved having a home remodel or a project to work on together. It was such a connecting, bonding thing for us. We were go-getters who liked to crush life, so what do we do with ourselves when there's nothing left to master?

We were happy with our home and our new lives here, but we felt a little itch and we weren't sure what it meant. Instead of feeling discontented or being reactionary, we waited. We leaned into God and sought wisdom on what that feeling might be telling us. We were okay with the sitting and the waiting. We didn't love it—it absolutely killed us to be still. But we'd gotten good at it during our seventeen months of living in the trailer, waiting for the house that would never be built. We've learned that the fruit that comes from waiting and seeking after what God wants for us is worth the discomfort of the pause.

So we waited and asked God, "What's next?"

D While work required a large mental investment, the company encouraged everyone to live balanced lives, which was shocking to me, coming out of my previous job. I had never worked for a company like this. That kind of freedom motivated me to be really intentional about my time at the office. I became significantly more productive in fewer hours. The chaos of moving to the Bay Area slowly faded, and a calm started to settle in.

Except for one thing.

Remember the piece of land we'd bought in Southern California and never built on? The dirt pile with the Japanese beetles and weeds? Yeah, before we moved north, we put that land up for sale, hoping that someone would quickly snatch up the money pit we'd called home for seventeen months. No go. It still sat there, unsold, taunting us. It was the biggest financial stressor in our lives, for sure.

Each week, Ash would inquire, "Any news on SoCal?" To which I would reply, "Nope."

That stupid land was slowly draining us financially.

I had done my best to give that property over to God, knowing that at the right time, it would sell. But after a year, it still hadn't sold. Not a single offer! I started to get angry. In the hot market of Southern California, how was this even possible? We had dropped the price four times, and its current listing price would mean a loss of almost $200,000—and that was if the buyer gave us what we were asking. I was becoming bitter over how much that land had taken from us.

I complained to Ash over dinner one night. "Baby, all the money we made from the sale of our first house is gone, along with the bonus money I got for staying loyal to my previous company."

"I know," she said. "This land is killing me! We need it to sell."

We went back and forth, complaining about everything we had hated about the land—the bugs, the dirt, the poop, a neighbor who'd tried to block us from building. I wanted so badly to get rid of that land and forget about it forever.

> *The fruit that comes from waiting and seeking after what God wants for us is worth the discomfort of the pause.*

"You know," Ash reminded me, "what about what the land gave us?"

"What?" I said. "That land gave us nothing but trouble for more than a year and a half!"

"Hear me out," she said. "That land was the biggest blessing that ever happened to us. I don't think we would be us without it. Yes, we lost money, but we found contentment there. We got my career out of it. All of our prior marriage issues were brought to light and slowly, one by one, cleaned up and fixed."

She was right. The land might have come with a hefty price tag financially, but what we gained was priceless. Seeing the land through Ash's eyes, I was able to let go of the anger, bitterness, and most of all, the sense of failure I realized I had been carrying over never building on that land and not being able to sell it.

The week after that conversation, someone called with an all-cash offer. At long last, it sold.

be intentional about
filling your space

We found a sofa for the tiny family room in our bungalow soon after we'd moved in, but for the life of me, I could not find a coffee table to go with it. The room was an odd shape, and due to the layout of windows and doorways, the only place for a table was right near the front door. It needed to be the perfect size, color, style—and price. I wanted a deal! And I was willing to wait.

But whenever I shared photos of our family room with no coffee table on my Instagram, people would take one look at that empty hole and begin questioning my design decisions.

"Why aren't you getting a coffee table?" they'd ask. Or "You really should get a coffee table for that area." My in-box was filled with these slightly stabbing questions and statements. But I didn't allow them to pressure me. I'd simply respond, "I'm waiting for the perfect piece." I felt content in that decision.

And let me tell you, did it pay off! Eight months after moving in, I stumbled upon a super-duper random sale at Anthropologie, and not only did I get the perfect coffee table, I got that quality piece at 60 percent off the original price. All because I waited.

QUICK TIPS

▶ Gather fresh ideas from magazines and online sites.

▶ Take your sweet time to settle on choices.

▶ Leave breathing room for a sense of peace.

BE INTENTIONAL ABOUT FILLING YOUR SPACE

Here are three tips to help you be patient as you fill your home with pieces you love.

>>> **Gather fresh ideas.** Fill your head with new visions of what your space could become. Just because you've always had a coffee table in your living room, for example, doesn't mean you need to continue having one. Just because you've always played it safe with traditional furniture doesn't mean you can't change gears and go modern. Browse through home-design magazines for inspiration. Spend an afternoon scrolling through Pinterest and Instagram to see what others have done. Create a Pinterest folder for each project and fill it with your favorite concepts and looks. Think of it as a mood board for your undertaking, and don't be afraid to use these ideas as a springboard for your own creativity.

>>> **Take your sweet time.** Go slowly and choose wisely. Sounds boring, especially when you're so excited to redo and fill a new home or an empty space. But trust me, friend, it's way more satisfying to wait for what you really want. Over time, you'll be able to walk around your home and feel great about everything your eye sees. Your home will become a place that reflects your unique style, a place you truly love.

>>> **Leave breathing room.** I love to leave an empty wall, corner, or space on my mantel. I'd rather look at a bare white wall than one filled with clutter and chaos that only cause me stress.

An empty place creates visual breathing room. It creates peace. Remember, less is more. Cramming in too many "perfect pieces" equals too much stuff.

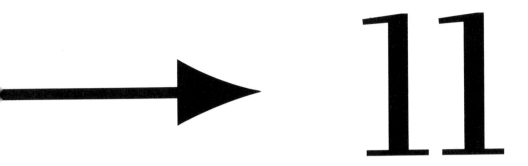

11

the pancake challenge
and the upward spiral

By early December, our little Spanish bungalow was already decorated for the holidays. I'd used simple twinkle lights, candles, and decor I'd gathered from nature, a skill I'd honed during our Christmases in the trailer. It kept the home feeling light and festive rather than heavy and overburdened with Santa stuff.

There was another trailer tradition we wanted to keep going. We were still riding high on our wave of gifting experiences over things. In that vein, Dino came to me with an idea that has come to be known as the Pancake Challenge.

D It was a genius plan, just saying. To fully understand how this went down, you need to know something about my wife: She loves food. Not just a little. A lot. I don't know anyone who appreciates the sense of taste as much as Ash does. She loves home-cooked dinners, meals with friends, coffee shops, restaurants. In her own words: "I love food. I love the taste of it, and I love the experience of enjoying it with people I cherish. Seeing someone else eating a brownie feels like a gift to me. I know I'm an odd cat, but food with friends really brings me joy."

Back to my genius plan. Our conversation went something like this.

Me: Okay, hear me out: You love food and I love sex, right?

Ash: Absolutely. You know it.

Me: Well, for Christmas this year, how about for one whole week, I make you food. I will cook or prepare anything you want in the kitchen, 24/7. I will anticipate your every food want or need, and then sit down and eat it with you.

Ash: Anything?

Me: Anything. Meals, snacks, desserts—all of it. The ideal scenario is you won't even have to ask or tell me your cravings. I will spend every waking minute thinking about what culinary adventure I can take you on throughout the day.

Ash: And . . . ?

Me: And . . . in return, you'll do the same for me at night, but with all things "sexy time." Back rubs, foot massages, lingerie, dancing. I dunno—use your imagination. A whole week of great, fun sex. Physical affection and intimacy, all the way.

Ash: I'm in! Love it.

Me: You sure?

Ash: Absolutely! The idea that you would cook anything I want and sit down to eat with me whenever I want is like a dream come true. Brilliant. And the sex, too!

Me: Fantastic!

Ash: What if I crave pancakes at 2 a.m.?

Me: Then pancakes it is! But what if I want 2 a.m. "pancakes"? You okay with that?

Ash: *(raising a fist in the air)* Babe, if you want "pancakes" at 2 a.m., I'm so in.

So we agreed to no gift buying that year. Just loving each other in really tangible ways.

And we had so much fun that week. My mind was constantly focused on my wife. What new thing could I make for her? What was she in the mood for? What could I do in the kitchen that would really wow her?

Of course, if I'm completely honest, I wanted to set a high bar on my end during the day so she'd feel motivated to maximize the late-night fun.

I was really feeling this challenge. I was on board from the get-go, and Dino did not disappoint. Every single day, he put so much thought and intention into serving me through food.

"Okay, babe, what do you want for breakfast, lunch, and dinner?" he'd ask each morning. Then he'd plan the day's meals accordingly. If I was sitting on the sofa, working, he'd pop over and ask, "Can I make you a snack? What are you in the mood for?" Or I'd pass him in the kitchen where tantalizing smells were coming from the oven and he'd announce, "I'm planning an amazing dessert for tonight!" I mean, he really went above and beyond on every single detail. *For a whole week.*

"If you keep this up, babe," I told him, rubbing my full belly after an especially amazing dessert, "I'll be looking like Mrs. Claus by next Christmas!"

I held up my end of the deal at first. Dino loves sex, but he also finds a ton of connection through other types of physical affection, so I tried to be intentional about kissing him on the cheek whenever I walked by, holding his hand while we walked through the mall, or simply rubbing his arm while we were cuddling on the sofa watching television. I made sure that whenever he wanted something physically—from neck rubs to sex—I'd do my part to meet his desires.

The Pancake Challenge was actually so much fun that when the week was over, we regrouped and agreed to keep it going for a whole month. I poured myself into all things kitchen. I found amazing recipes online and discovered that I genuinely loved doing this for Ash. Our kids loved the incredible meals—and especially the desserts. Everyone was happy.

I'm Italian, although I don't speak a lick of the language or even enjoy pasta. But my wife loves a good fettuccini. How hard could it be to make pasta, am I right? So one Saturday, I corralled Quinn, age six, into being my sous-chef—I think it's *aiuto cuoco* in Italian—and we set about making fettuccini for the family.

I didn't have any fancy pasta-making tools, but I did own a Cuisinart food processor, a rolling pin, and a broom. I found a recipe online and we dove in.

We blended the dough in the Cuisinart, then Quinn and I took turns kneading the ball of dough until it felt velvety smooth. "It's like Play-Doh, Daddy!" she said.

Next came rolling the dough flat. Hand-rolling pasta dough is a good upper-body workout, let me tell you. Once it was about a quarter of an inch thick, we rolled it up and I cut it into half-inch slices. Quinn unrolled the spirals of fettuccini and hung them across a broom handle, which we suspended from the kitchen island to the counter.

After hanging the last piece of fettuccini, Quinn stood back. "Now, *that's* Italian!" she said, touching her fingertips to her mouth, kissing them, then flaring them upward like an old-soul Italian chef.

That night Ashley and the kids enjoyed fettuccini marinara, with pasta made by me and my pint-sized, curly-haired *aiuto cuoco*. I got husband points from Ash—and Daddy points from Quinn. I love how the kitchen creates a great atmosphere for making family memories together.

Dino was rocking his part of the Pancake Challenge, but as the month wore on, I wasn't nearly as attentive. I wasn't asking Dino what he wanted. I wasn't seeking to please him as much as he was seeking to please me. I simply figured a few affectionate touches during the day and sex at night would check all the right boxes. I was simply going through the motions, doing what I thought would make Dino happy without ever checking in with him or asking him what would make him feel most loved.

All the while, he was going above and beyond for me, going out of his way with so much love and intention in the kitchen.

I continued to flex my creative muscles in the kitchen as I found new ways to serve my wife. I discovered this love for food and cooking that I had no idea was inside me. I loved spending time after work researching correct cooking techniques and learning which flavors paired well with others. I was finding so much joy in it for myself, and Ash seemed more than happy to reap the rewards of my growing hobby.

I'd love to report that my new joy of cooking and my selflessness as a husband were the whole picture. But nope. Down deep, I was also hoping that Ash would see the amount of effort I was putting into my half of the Pancake Challenge and I'd get the same effort from her in return. I'd imagined that somehow, I wouldn't even have to ask for what I wanted when it came to sex, that she would be able to read my mind like I was trying to read her mind with food.

I had unspoken expectations, and when they weren't met, I felt hurt. The more hurt I felt, the more I allowed resentment and disappointment to build up.

Let me clue you in on a little shocker: People can't read our minds.

I am a very bad communicator on all things feelings. Both because of my natural wiring and some hurtful experiences I had growing up, I had been shoving my own feelings deep, deep down from an early age. I didn't want to let them bubble up to the surface now. *No feelings, no hurt.*

It had taken me a long time to understand this unhelpful trait in myself. Luckily, I have an amazingly gracious wife who adores me, who moves toward me when I'm feeling hurt and encourages me to explore my emotions. She lets me talk it out. We now have this nice rhythm where she just lets me speak and then asks questions to help me figure out what I'm actually feeling—even when she is the one who hurt me.

It took a full month of bottling up my feelings before Ash finally called me out.

"Babe, it feels like these past couple of weeks, you keep harping on me for little stuff," she said one Saturday after a big breakfast of—ironically—pancakes. "Is something bugging you? What's going on?"

And once again, Ash worked her magic, coaxing my feelings to the surface in her gentle way. We had a long conversation about where each of us had succeeded—and failed—in the Pancake Challenge. And the more I verbalized what I'd been feeling, the more I could see how unfair my expectations were—and how Dino-centric my motivations to serve my wife had been. *Crap.*

Even though all my cooking and baking made it look like I was showing love to my wife, I was doing so mostly out of selfishness. I had secretly engaged Ash in a barter system dependent on fair trade rather than a giving system rooted in selfless sacrifice. I gave to Ash and expected something in return. When I didn't get it, I felt ripped off and hurt.

My part in the Pancake Challenge should have been to *give* to Ash, no strings attached. But I had been expecting something in return—more physical intimacy.

"Babe, I'm so sorry for all the silent expectations I put on you," I told her. "So unfair. And I am so, so sorry for how my little resentments leaked out and polluted this experience."

"Hey," she replied, "I'm just as much to blame. Once we extended the Challenge to a month, eventually I just started checking boxes. We both have room for improvement, but I still say the Pancake Challenge is a huge win. A few tweaks needed, but a win!"

Serving the other person must come without strings attached, without expectation.

We both realized we were a little lacking in a vital component to this game: selflessness. Serving the other person must come without strings attached, without expectation. Otherwise, it's not serving. It's bartering.

I was just as guilty as Dino of having selfish motives. I felt so loved by those amazing meals and desserts, but I hadn't been nearly as interested in making sure Dino felt loved. My focus had been on getting, not giving.

The Pancake Challenge was a keeper, for sure. We just needed to check in with each other regularly to make sure our motive remained fixed on caring for the other person.

 We have since done and redone this challenge, and I still struggle to keep my focus on giving, not getting. In fact, that tension is now why I do it. It forces me to be attentive to "no strings attached."

Ash is just naturally less selfish than I am. She has her issues as we all do, but overall, I'm much more likely to reflexively put my needs first. As you know by now, I spent years intentionally trying to prune this behavior. That discipline is real and ongoing. Selfishness comes naturally to me, so I try to push away from that tendency by serving my wife and kids without expecting something in return. That way (1) I'm not disappointed, and (2) I'm serving for the right reason.

We don't become less selfish by getting more but by giving more. This one insight has perhaps been most transformative in shaping me into who I am today.

I have yet to meet someone whose inner thirst to be loved was quenched by drinking from the cup of self. While my human nature is naturally self-centered, I don't have to stay that way. I have choices. I can fight this tendency, and the Pancake Challenge (with the right motivation) has been a really fun way to rein in my own selfish tendencies.

We don't become less selfish by getting more, but by giving more.

upward spiral

After a few more rounds of the Pancake Challenge, we started to look for other ways of gamifying our relationship. When Dino came to me a few weeks later with a new challenge, I was all ears.

Earlier that spring while hanging out with a buddy, I listened as he began to unload about the hard time he was having in his marriage.

"She is just the worst right now," he'd said of his wife. "I'm giving everything and getting nothing in return but nagging and more nagging . . ."

On and on he went. I did my best to be a sympathetic listener (the kind of friend I wanted when my investment went south). I asked a few questions, but to be honest, this buddy wasn't interested in talking either about constructive solutions or about possible contributions he might have been making to their problems. He just wanted to vent.

I get it. It feels good in the moment to have a buddy agree about how much your spouse sucks and how you are just one great big hero, but it's not helpful. In fact, it's harmful. As I tried to be his sounding board, the guy worked himself into a toxically negative view of his wife, whom I knew to be a pretty great woman.

I thought back to a recent Saturday when Ash and I had been picking at each other all day long. No big blowup, just little jabs. I wasn't that different from this guy. My thoughts toward my wife had gotten sucked into a negative tailspin too.

That chat with my friend gave me an idea for a new game with Ash. That evening before bed, I hit her up.

"Let's play another marriage game," I said.

"I dunno," she teased. "You set a pretty high bar for yourself with the Pancake Challenge. I'm not sure you can top it. A new game needs to be at least as good as the last one."

"Here's what I propose—and first, a little backstory," I said before telling her about listening to my buddy all evening. "Remember last weekend when you and I were snappy at each other all day long?"

"Um, let's see," Ash said. "Yeah, I def remember you being super picky about every little thing I did, while I responded sweetly, like the perfect angel that I always am. Is that how you remember it?"

"Oh, exactly," I said. "We recall that day *exactly the same*."

We laughed.

"Seriously, though," I continued, "we sort of fell into a real downward spiral that day."

"Yeah, not our finest performance," she agreed. "But what's your game idea?"

"What if we both spend a whole week being hyperintentional about doing the same thing, but with positive stuff toward each other instead of negative? What if, instead of getting sucked into a downward spiral, we created one in reverse?"

"Like an upward spiral! I love it!" Ash said. "So no picking at each other? Only positive input? But how do we measure that? How do I win?"

"It's more than no picking," I said. "Deeper than that. For me, my negative words don't come out of nowhere. They start as critical thoughts. I get irritated about something and dwell on it. Those thoughts fester until they tumble out as words, and then my words become actions. Same for you?"

"Definitely."

"So for this game, you and I will spend each day being super aware of—and intentional about—the thoughts we think about each other and the positive words we then speak to each other. Ideally, we'll let that overflow into the positive ways we treat each other. It'll be sort of an experiment. How quickly can our thoughts change our words, and our words change our actions? We're trying to create an upward spiral—and most of the work for both of us will be in our thoughts and words. My theory is that the action part will come easy if we root ourselves in positive thoughts and words."

As I listened to Dino's story about his buddy's venting about his wife, two images flashed into my mind:

First, I recalled those wise words Chelsea had spoken during my women's Bible study so many years ago: "What kind of thoughts do you think about your husband? Do you cherish him?" Ever since, I'd tried to implement them into my view of my husband, and I'd seen the positive effect of this on Dino.

This Upward Spiral game would take it to an even deeper level. My thoughts about Dino could lead to affirming words, which would then create positive actions. It had the power to change how I actually felt toward him.

Second, I thought about that night when I'd gone out with my girlfriends and it had turned into husband bashing. How quickly that conversation had become a downward spiral, so much so that I'd left in tears. Could positive thoughts and words truly create a powerful upward spiral? I was dang curious to find out.

Since the start of our Pancake Challenge, Dino had been practicing this same mentality of cherishing me that I tried to live out toward him. I could feel the love and effort he was putting forth, and I really did feel so cherished. I knew I hadn't put in as much effort to make him feel loved during the Pancake Challenge. Now I had a second chance. I had such a desire to return love and affection to my husband, putting aside my selfish tendencies and seeking after whatever would bring him joy.

For a full week, Dino and I crushed the Upward Spiral game. I was determined to focus on my own thoughts, words, and actions, not keep score of what Dino was or wasn't doing. And he did the exact same for me.

≫ Gamify Your Relationship ≪

Make personal growth a little more fun by gamifying your relationship. You can give the Pancake Challenge or Upward Spiral a try or make up a game of your own. Here are the only two ground rules:

1. Winning equals making things better for the other person, not for yourself.
2. Each person focuses on their own progress or growth, not on that of the other person.

It wasn't as hard as it sounds. I just got into the habit of speaking the positive things I noticed him doing, and getting specific about what I appreciated, like this: "Thanks for doing the dinner dishes with the boys. The kitchen looks fantastic!"

Or this: "I am so grateful for how hard you work at Netflix. Your income gives me the freedom to expand my business from home."

Or this: "Gosh, babe, you're lookin' so fit in that tank top. I'm digging the results of your commitment to better health."

Dino started doing the same for me. Within the first few days, we could both sense a shift in our attitudes, a lightness in how we related with each other, and a dramatic increase in—my favorite word—joy. This created a natural upward spiral of positive behavior in our marriage. I could feel it, Dino could feel it, and incredibly, even our kids could feel it. They started mirroring the same kind of positive words and actions toward each other. So cool to see!

Others-focused sacrifice isn't an easy thing. But even with our imperfect attempts at the Pancake Challenge and this Upward Spiral game, our kids saw each parent selflessly put the other person ahead of themselves, and it felt good to know they were taking note.

As Christ followers, Dino and I do our best to model for our kids the kind of love Jesus modeled, which was a serving-others love. The Upward Spiral game provided a real-time example for how they could treat each other—and any future spouses—with selflessness. They saw a husband serving his wife and a wife serving her husband—imperfectly, I might add. And not without bumps. But we'll take it.

We'd spent the past few years living in tight quarters; first in the trailer and now in the Spanish bungalow. One of the unexpected blessings of being crammed together was that it forced Dino and me to work out our differences rather than isolate from each other. We got to practice what it looks like to love authentically and sacrificially. How deeply we needed the lessons these homes taught us. No matter what our next seasons hold, we're packing those lessons along for the ride.

decorating for any holiday

The holiday season of the Pancake Challenge and the Upward Spiral game will always stand out in my mind, not only for what it taught us about serving each other, but because it was our first Christmas in a traditional home after living in the trailer. I loved that we maintained our value of experience-focused gifts beyond the trailer, but what about decorating? Now that I was in a traditional home once again, I was free to go crazy and decorate, right?

Nope. My love for simplicity outweighed my love for holiday decorating. November and December can be a crazy and stressful time. Eliminating the strain of overdecorating your home is a great way to start the season fresh and enjoy it with a clear mind.

This principle applies for any holiday, not just Christmas. I used to own bins of slightly likable holiday decor, stuff I'd bought at 80 percent off after the holidays. I'd open up box after box, hoping to get into the holiday spirit, but instead of feeling excited, I felt overwhelmed. *Where am I gonna put all this junk?*

Each time we moved I pruned my collection of holiday decorations, and I'd finally whittled it down to one or two bins of our favorite things.

QUICK TIPS

▶ Pull from nature.
▶ Pull from your own home.

▶ Maximize ambience by engaging all five senses.

My discipline of asking specific questions ("Do I need it, love it, or have room for it?") helped me wade through all those decorations. Now every item in those bins brings me sheer joy. There are memories attached to each item, and stories too.

But our small number of beloved decorations didn't make enough of an impact to create the holiday spirit I was looking for in our new 1,300-square-foot home. What to do?

In the trailer, I'd relied heavily on nature to create ambience inside our walls. I applied the same principle here. Then I pulled out things I already had around the house, like a red tablecloth that works for Valentine's Day, Independence Day, and Christmas; and a plain white serving platter I placed beneath a center-piece of red candles and a handful of greenery that I snipped from the hedges in our yard.

DECORATING FOR ANY HOLIDAY

This approach excites me because it allows for more flexibility and creativity. Inspire yourself with these decorating ideas that require little to no year-round storage.

⋙ **Pull from nature.** I love foraging in my backyard for plants, flowers, pine cones, acorns, and sticks that can add to the decor of any particular season. Even if you don't think you have an eye for flower arranging, you can place an assortment of them in a vase and it will look great. I promise, you'll be surprised by how easy it is.

If you have a mantel, a wide windowsill, or open shelving, place some sprigs of green along its length as your base, and then plop a few red berries or pine cones randomly throughout as focal points. Use odd rather than even numbers for your focal points (three candles, not two, or five pine cones, not six, for example), because odd numbers of items are more aesthetically pleasing. Stand back, assess, then tweak as needed. There is something so peaceful about bringing nature into your home. And the fresh aroma of outdoors just smells like an old-fashioned holiday.

If you live in a condo or apartment without a yard, check out Costco and Trader Joe's. They're a great source for the fall and winter seasons, offering inexpensive greenery, flowers, pumpkins, cinnamon sticks, and more. Even grocery stores carry cinnamon-scented pine cones this time of year. Christmas tree lots also offer good prices on fir or pine branches that make great centerpieces, bouquets, or garland.

⋙ **Pull from your own home.** Every season I change out my bed's duvet cover with one that matches the colors of that season. It's a fun way to decorate without actually buying holiday decor. I love keeping pillow covers in a few different colors on hand as well. When a new season comes along, I can simply swap out to a color I feel best represents that season. During fall, I pull out my rust-colored pillow covers. Red ones work for Christmas, Valentine's Day, and even Independence Day.

Although this means I'm storing a small handful of covers during the off months, they don't take up much space, and they add to my home's coziness without adding clutter. I also love that they work for more than one purpose or season.

Candles, too, come in a variety of colors and scents. Choosing colors and aromas that match the holiday or time of year makes my whole kitchen or living room feel festive. Burning through the candles by the end of that season means I don't have to store them.

These simple touches make a statement without feeling over-whelming. They make my home feel cozy without the stress of knowing everything needs to be stored in the dreaded bins for another eleven months once the holiday is over.

>>> **Maximize ambience by engag-ing all five senses.** When planning to decorate for holidays or special events, don't limit yourself to what others will see. Think of what they'll hear, touch, smell, and taste as well. By triggering all five senses, you'll create an atmosphere your friends and family will never forget.

- **See.** I love to be able to walk into a room and know instantly what season we're in simply by the colors. Pillows, a vase of flowers, or a colored jar candle is all it takes. It's okay to get a little cre-ative with the traditional colors too. Add a little purple and green to Halloween, or blue and gold to Christmas. Maybe mix a few fuchsia or orange flowers into a traditional red Valentine's bouquet or some burgundy into a Thanksgiving centerpiece.

  Another easy way to use the sense of sight in your decorating is through lighting. Swap out a white porch light bulb for a green one at Christmastime. If replacing old string lights, consider buying multi-color lights with remotes that allow you to display a different color each holiday, as well as white for year-round use.

- **Smell.** The scent of candles can quickly bring back a memory or feeling of nostalgia. One of my favorite money-saving tricks is reusing an Anthropologie or Yankee Candles candle jar. After the original candle is used up, I drop in a more affordable pillar candle from Trader Joe's, which plops perfectly right in the middle as if they were made for each other—and for about one-eighth the price of replacing the original candle. I like to stock up on my favorite scents, especially ones we associate with certain holidays, such as pumpkin spice, pine, fir, spruce, sugar cookie, cinnamon, or gingerbread.

  Baking is another way to really target the sense of smell. I love walking into a home that has something yummy going on in the oven, don't you? Even if you're not a master chef, you can use the kitchen to your advantage. Fill a saucepan with apple juice, then toss in some cinnamon, cloves, and nutmeg. Instant Christmas potpourri that you can drink!

- **Hear.** We always have music playing throughout our home. Dino is a big fan of playing music in the background regardless of what we're doing. Turn on your favorite playlist and relax to the sounds of the season—not just Christmas tunes, but whatever songs fit different times of the year. Play beach tunes in the summer, jazz in the fall—whatever style of music your family loves. By being intentional about playing the same type of music each season, you create instant ambience for their ears.

- **Taste.** Favorite holiday recipes create lasting memories, especially for kids.

  I'm a terrible baker and cook, but even I can put some store-bought cookie-dough slices onto a sheet. Think through what flavors your family members associate with each holiday, and then bring their taste buds to life.

  You don't need to make stuff from scratch to maximize taste. And you don't need to stick with traditional menus. Maybe eating at a Chinese buffet on New Year's has become a beloved tradition for your fam. Or maybe you eat pizza instead of grilled hot dogs on Independence Day. Great! Roll with it.

- **Touch.** A cozy faux fur blanket or pillow never hurt anybody, that's all I'm saying. Snuggly textures just make me want to sink deeper into a sofa and enjoy a cup of something warm with someone I love. Soft goods add a cozy element to your sofa, tables, and chairs. They're like people magnets, enticing your friends and family to want to stay for hours.

  Keep a few lap quilts handy for the firepit outside, too. When the night gets chilly, you can add hours to that magical conversation by keeping everyone cozy with their own blanket.

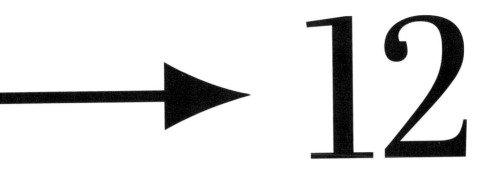

12

major expansion

I pray because I can't help myself. I pray because I'm helpless.
I pray because the need flows out of me all the time,
waking and sleeping. It doesn't change God. It changes me.

—ANTHONY HOPKINS AS C. S. LEWIS, *Shadowlands*

A fun bonus from our move to Northern California was that we now lived only twenty-five minutes from our friend (and Dino's former roommate) Greg and his wife, Hillary. Dino and Greg worked together at Netflix.

One night we headed to their house for dinner. Side note: I love being invited over to friends' houses for dinner. I love the relational connection, the laughter, the good food. Dinner with Greg and Hillary would be a real treat.

Walking into their adorable Victorian home always inspired me. Hillary has such a unique eye for design, and she had added her personal touch everywhere I looked. It was like walking into a magazine. Plus, she's an incredible cook, so I'm always hit with a blast of yumminess as soon as I walk in.

This time, Dino and I were hit with something else too: the sweet sound of their brand-new baby boy. We were clearly done with having babies at this point. A bunch of older kids and a vasectomy will do that to you.

But as we wined and dined with Greg and Hillary that evening, I couldn't take my eyes off them and their little son. Hillary is such a relaxed and stress-free mama. This baby was her third, and she had it down. She draped a blanket over her shoulder and discreetly nursed the baby, not breaking stride as we visited. Then she curled him up on the sofa. He was only a few weeks old and wasn't rolling over yet, but just in case she tucked a blanket around him, keeping him snug and secure as we moved to the dining table. I loved that she kept him nearby as we enjoyed our meal.

That stress-free vibe is a gift that seems to come after you've done motherhood a few times. It brought back such great memories. Every time I'd hear little squeaks and grunts coming from that bundle of joy on the sofa, my heart felt a little tug. *What is that about?*

Without much thought, I blurted out, "We should have another baby, Dino."

Everyone at the dinner table stopped midchew and stared.

"Yes! Do it!" Greg and Hillary chimed in.

"Nope!" said Dino, making a scissors sign to remind everyone he'd had a vasectomy years before.

We all just laughed and let it go. That was that.

Months went by, and those wonderful dinners with Greg and Hillary continued. Every time we saw them, the topic of Dino and me having another baby would somehow work its way into the conversation. Mind you, I didn't even really want another baby. This wasn't one of those things I was begging Dino for and then arguing about with him at home. But it kept coming up in conversation. And I wasn't the only one bringing it up. Dino would too. The baby topic seemed to teeter-totter between Dino and me every time we saw Greg and Hillary and that sweet baby of theirs.

sophie and james plus two strangers

D Greg and Hillary's baby definitely got Ash and me joking about having another one of our own, but we weren't even a little bit serious about it. We were happy with our family of five and were very grateful for our three successful pregnancies. Our earlier miscarriage forever heightened our appreciation for the miracle of a new baby. But the idea kept resurfacing.

Then some new friends, Sophie and James, invited us to an outdoor chef's dinner at their winery, which bore their names. The dinner was like nothing we'd ever experienced: dozens of people gathered around one massive, one-hundred-foot-long table, set low to the ground, that overlooked Sonoma Valley from the winery's mountaintop perch. The table itself was a work of art, made out of rough-hewn slabs of wood. Everyone sat on giant pillows or throw rugs, drinking wine and eating the most amazing food. With the Sophie James winery all around us and San Pablo Bay in the distance, the view was just stunning. Ash and I sat there, soaking it all in.

Late in the evening, Ash struck up a conversation with the couple seated next to me, inquiring about their jobs and family—the usual.

"Do you guys have kids?" the wife asked.

"Yep! We have three, ages nine, seven, and five," Ash informed her. "Boy, boy, girl."

"Oh, such great ages! Are you all done?" the wife asked.

"Yep!" I butted in, raising my finger scissors proudly to the sky. "I got the snip while Ash was still pregnant with Quinn."

Ash laughed and nodded that it was true. She had long ago stopped trying to change the fact that I share too much personal information with strangers. Then Sophie stopped by and waved Ash into another conversation.

The wife turned to me. "You know, you can get that reversed," she said, making scissor fingers in the air.

"Shhh!" I said, laughing. "Don't encourage her! She might hear you!"

"Can I tell you a story?" she asked.

"Sure."

"Years ago, some friends of ours did just what you and Ashley did: After their third baby, they got a vasectomy. But then they changed their minds and decided to go for another round of kiddos. The husband went under the knife to have his vasectomy reversed, and it worked. They had two more kids, six years after their last baby."

"And?" I asked, my curiosity getting the better of me.

"Best decision they ever made. To hear them describe it, the older kids have been so blessed by the younger ones and, of course, the littler ones have these incredible older siblings to look up to. There's this amazing dynamic in their family."

"We've met their kids," added the husband, "so we've seen it first-hand. For them, it's turned out to be a beautiful thing."

Hmm. Interesting.

"You two are a bad influence!" I joked. "And you definitely aren't allowed to talk to my wife for the rest of the evening!"

But their words hung in my mind. Up until this point, I hadn't seriously considered having more kids—under any circumstance. Hard stop. Period. End of conversation. I was older now. I was happy with the current phase our kids were in. No diaper bag, no plastic pouches of breast milk filling the freezer. I loved that my wife and I had the freedom to run off and do whatever we wanted, whenever we wanted. Ash and I had worked so hard on our marriage, and I didn't want to start over with the newborn stage.

But from that random conversation with total strangers, had a tiny seed been planted?

Nope. Not happening.

> *From a random conversation with total strangers, had a tiny seed been planted?*

It had been seven months of this on-again, off-again, back-and-forth crazy talk between Dino and me about the idea of trying for another baby. I felt like it had become serious enough that we needed to resolve this thing.

"Let's just pray about it," I said to Dino one morning over coffee. Ha! Basically, a spiritual trump card. How could he say no to that? He's a firm believer in prayer.

"Okay, fair enough," he said.

After years of practice, I had learned never to force something with Dino, especially a topic as life changing as adding another child to our family. We'd pray about it, reach an aligned decision, and then figure it out.

Over the past fifteen years—through Las Vegas, a big house, little houses, and even a trailer—Dino and I had developed a deep trust in one another, and an even deeper trust in God's plans over our own. We both wanted whatever He wanted with this baby idea.

To be honest, I wasn't even sure how I felt about it. Though I was still uncertain, I was leaning more yes than no. It would mean going through another pregnancy—and this one in my thirties. But poor Dino! For him, it would mean heading to the doctor's office to have his vasectomy reversed.

I asked God, *Are we crazy? Is this really Your plan for us? Are we seriously supposed to consider having another baby? Life is so sweet right now. Like, we're in the prime of our lives. Financially stable, in a home we remodeled and love. And both of us have jobs that we absolutely adore.*

And just a reminder, God, our kids are now old enough to wipe themselves, feed themselves, sleep through the night, and swim. They do chores. They shower. They can even make a sandwich. Why would anyone mess with all of that goodness?

But dang it. That tugging in my heart continued, so I dug deeper. *Are You inviting us to examine our lifestyle and intentions? Hmmm. Well, what are Dino and I building? What do we want our future to look like in five years? In ten? What does it mean to be the Petrone family?*

I always looked forward to bedtime with our kids. Each child's routine consisted of a little one-on-one time with Dad or Mom, and then we prayed together before lights-out. I loved spending a little time with each kid, just letting them have some individual attention and a chance to discuss anything they wanted.

We'd not included the kids in our process of considering adding a baby to our family. This was a grown-up decision. But one night when I went to tuck Quinn in, I found her crying in her room.

"What's wrong, love?" I asked.

"Daddy, I just wish I had a baby sister," she said.

What?

"Sorry, baby girl, that's just not gonna happen," I said, wiping her tears

and stroking her curly head. "I don't want to give you false hope."

"But what if I prayed and asked God for a sister?" she asked.

Oh boy. She was bringing God into it too. "Quinn, if you really want this, of course you can pray and ask God to give you a sister. But keep in mind, God is not a magic lamp. You don't always get what you want just because you prayed. Sometimes God says no. If I were you, I'd also pray that if God isn't going to give you a sister, He'll soften your desire for one. Maybe He has something different in mind for you."

Boom. Dad of the Year, right there. Another learning moment for the little girl. A quick kiss on the head, and then off I went to hang out with my wife. Surely this would be the end of it.

I came to Dino one evening and asked, "What are we working toward, babe?"

"Huh?" he asked. "What do you mean?"

"Well, we literally don't need a thing at this point in our lives. We can do whatever we want. We can travel easily, with or without the kids. We can be generous with others. If we save and invest wisely, we might even be able to retire around the time the boys start moving out of the house. It sounds like everything we had dreamed of, but is that what we want?"

I was genuinely interested in his answer—and even my own. Did we want a life that was comfortable, with everything the world said we needed for happiness?

Dino stared at me, a little stunned. "Wow, that's the question," he said. "Our lives are so comfortable. The problem is, we don't really like comfort."

"I know!" I said. "Nothing ever feels good to us about being comfortable. We're Petrones! We like a little edge in our lives."

"We like living in organized chaos," he added. "Obviously no one should have a baby just to create chaos . . ."

"No, no. Obviously. But we aren't the type to let the upheaval of a new baby stop us if that's the right decision."

"Exactly. We should decide this on what kind of future we want for our fam. What do we want Petrone-ness to look like in ten years?"

That conversation didn't answer the baby question, but it was clarifying. It helped us understand that if having another baby was the right decision, we would likely thrive with a little short-term chaos.

D I had underestimated my daughter. Quinn began praying for a baby sister every night. *Every. Single. Night.* I'd go in, pray with her, and give her a kiss. As I walked out, I could hear her little voice praying, "Please, God, bring me a little sister of my very own." *Ugh. This was getting tough.*

Driving to work, I prayed about the baby idea, still feeling confident this was a no, not a yes. I wrestled back and forth. *God, is this just another of Ash's and my wild ideas? Let's face it, we're both the type to get excited about change and challenge, but most of the time, our excitement fizzles once we stop to think about it from all angles. Is this just that?*

If I'm supposed to do this baby thing, You need to change my heart. I don't wanna. I like to have a plan, and I like to work that plan. Well, this current plan is working. Why mess with it? No chance I'm letting my plan get changed.

Ever heard the saying, "Want to make God laugh? Tell Him your plans"? Yeah. Me too.

As I continued driving toward work, a scene played out in my mind in which I was driving toward a fork in the road. In this scene, I recognized the path on the right. I knew it well. It was nicely paved, smooth, with neat, freshly painted yellow lines. The path on the left was a dirt road, wild, bumpy, and barely wide enough for my car.

You can go either way, Dino, I sensed God say. *The path you're on is fine. It's a good path. Turn right at the fork and you'll be comfortable. Enjoy it. But I do have a little more adventure for you if you choose to turn left.*

I knew what it would require of me to take that left fork. I knew I would need to surrender more of myself to go down that uncertain road and bring a fourth child into our family.

A new baby would mean sacrifice for both Ash and me. For me, it felt like I

> *If having another baby was the right decision, we would likely thrive with a little short-term chaos.*

would be giving up everything I had worked for to get our family to this point. To be totally honest, that selfish part of me was also fearful of losing Ash's attention to the baby. Losing her time, losing our intimacy, losing our freedom.

I had worked so incredibly hard to set up our lives in a specific way. We were in such a good place as a family! But at every significant point in my life thus far, whenever I'd chosen the path of sacrifice, I was a happier, more fulfilled man.

By the time I pulled into work, I was still uncertain which fork in the road to take. *God, You know I want to live a life that honors You with everything I do. But You'll need to soften my heart if this baby thing is the path You want me to take.*

Dino and I had an evening routine I absolutely loved. Once the kids were in bed, we snuggled down for the night too. We loved watching shows together in bed—not just zoning out in front of the TV but hitting pause a hundred times to laugh or talk about something while being all wrapped up around each other.

One such evening in October as we watched the credits roll on a rerun of *The Office*, Dino sat up. He hit pause, turned to me, and grabbed my hand. "Okay, what do you think about the name Fox?"

I knew exactly what he was talking about. The baby! He'd seen that name in the credits. "As a baby name? I love it so much!"

"Whether it's a boy or a girl, we could name it Fox?" he asked, just to be clear.

"Absolutely."

"Okay. Let's do it," he said. "I want to have another baby with you. Make the appointment for a reversal."

"Deal."

We'd been joking about it for seven months and praying about it in recent weeks. But the actual decision to expand our family all went down in the span of about seven seconds.

It might not make sense to anyone else, but for us, well, it worked. We'd even reached the decision without fighting! Progress.

Whether or not we'd succeed in creating another little Petrone remained to be seen.

two habits to keep you excited about your home

That dinner at Sophie James Wine Company turned out to be significant in our baby journey, but it was more than that. It inspired me in so many other ways as a designer. It got my creative juices flowing. With most of the home projects in our Spanish bungalow completed, I didn't want to slip into a comfortable groove. I wanted our little home to stay crisp, new-feeling, and cozy.

The truth is, once the creative fun of a move or a remodel is over, comfort can quickly turn into clutter, which then leaves us feeling overwhelmed, discontent, and stressed. So how do we continue to simplify, stay comfortable, and keep our homes feeling fresh?

BEFORE

AFTER

TWO HABITS TO KEEP YOU EXCITED ABOUT YOUR HOME

I've found two habits that serve me well when it comes to fighting clutter and complacency while keeping me excited about my home, even if there's no crazy remodel project on the horizon. See if they resonate with you.

>>> **Be observant.** Don't ever stop learning. Whenever you're at a friend's house, restaurant, gallery, store, or anywhere cool, take note of what you love about the design. Do their window dressings cascade into a beautiful pool of fabric on gleaming hardwood floors? Do they use herbs and acorns as a centerpiece? Have they left one wall entirely void of art or photos? If you love what they did, think how you could reproduce that look at home. Take a quick photo of whatever it is that appeals to you. Later you can unpack that inspiration and use it to freshen up the look of your own home.

The night at Sophie James gave me several new ideas. I hosted a dinner the following weekend, and instead of buying a bouquet of flowers as a centerpiece, I gathered dried grasses from alongside our road and arranged them in three spare coffee mugs, placing them randomly down the middle of the table, just as Sophie had done at the winery. Another time, I tried hosting a casual meal around our coffee table in the living room, using pillows and throw rugs instead of chairs. It was fun! Good ideas from others are worth adding to your own decor arsenal.

Obviously, the style of Sophie James Winery and the Sonoma Valley didn't match the design of my Spanish bungalow, but I still walked away from that mountaintop with tons of inspiration. (For one, how cool would it be to live in a vineyard? Ha!) But seriously, the simplicity of those table settings; the use of nature, raw wood, and soft goods (pillows and rugs) as furniture; the way everything outside was arranged to take advantage of the property's best views—all these choices were clearly intentional. And believe me, I took pictures! I tucked away plenty of new ideas for later use.

>>> **Develop a decluttering mindset.** Every few months I do a visual walk-through of our home, taking a mental inventory as I go. What have I brought into each room? Does it serve a purpose? Even if it does, is there simply too much stuff in this space?

I don't tackle the whole house at once, and I don't suggest you do either. The idea is to develop a rhythm so that you're constantly on the lookout for ways to eliminate clutter.

Start small. Maybe just tackle that one kitchen drawer—you know, the one where stuff just collects? That one. It's usually the messiest spot in the whole house, right? That's my favorite starting point because it feels so dang satisfying to clean it out. I can finish the whole drawer in about ten minutes. *Boom!* After that, I move on to another drawer or another room.

One area that deserves its own mention: the entryway. These are clutter magnets, especially if you have kids. Shoes, backpacks, coats, purses, umbrellas, and sports equipment seem to breed overnight at our house. What to do with all this stuff?

If you're lucky enough to have a garage entrance via a mudroom or laundry room, utilize that space to your advantage. I like to provide two labeled hooks per family member where they can hang coats or backpacks. Once their hooks are full, they have to store everything else in their rooms.

One friend of mine with five kids didn't have wall space for hooks, but she had a closet-sized freestanding cabinet. She solved the problem of too many coats in the closet by dedicating one wooden coat hanger to each person and then writing their name on it with permanent marker. Problem solved. Any extra coats

Three Questions for Eliminating Clutter

I can't stress enough how helpful these three questions are when it comes to deciding whether something should be kept or tossed. Here they are:

> **Do I need it?** If yes, keep. If no, bye-bye. Don't get too technical here. For example, art and decor aren't needs, but they add ambience to our homes.

> **Do I love it?** If yes, keep. If no, why not? Consider replacing it with something you'd love that serves the same purpose.

> **Do I have space for it?** If you need and love something but your drawer, closet, or room is too crowded, then something else must go. Bye-bye, something else.

got tossed into their owners' rooms. Shoes can go on a boot tray, storage bench, or shoe caddy. If you use a bin to store shoes by the door, make sure it has a top. Without a lid, the pile of shoes and boots inside the bin adds to visual clutter. With a lid, it adds to the feeling of simplicity and minimalism.

If your front-door entrance is your only pathway into the home, get creative about how to store those bulky items. Labeling is key, as is setting a limit on how many of each item a person can store in this prime real estate (the correct answer here is one or two items per person). Add a standing coat-rack for guests' jackets and use your entry closet to hide family clutter like coats, backpacks, umbrellas, and boots.

Don't forget to declutter your garage or basement, closets, kids' rooms, and outdoor spaces. When stuff piles up, it robs us of peace. Let your hunger for a peaceful home energize you as you work your way through your home, bit by bit.

Think beyond obvious clutter too. Look for what I call big clutter. Is the room mess-free but overcrowded? Are there too many pictures on the wall? Does it look a bit like a furniture warehouse?

Remember, too much of a good thing is too much of a good thing. Remove one piece of furniture or one wall hanging at a time until you feel yourself exhale as you look around the room. It should feel breezy and light, filling you with energy rather than angst.

I can't stress enough how much joy awaits you once you get on the other side of living with too much stuff. Tackle your clutter and defeat overcrowding. The air up here is wonderful. It's so much easier to breathe.

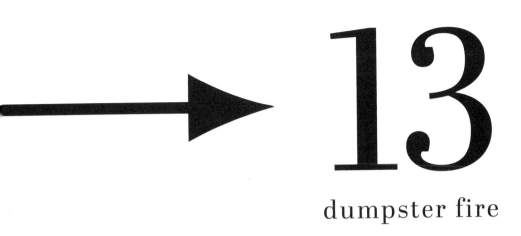

13

dumpster fire

Reversing a vasectomy is no small thing. The snip is not the same as the snap.[9] Like not even a little. Poor Dino! His original procedure took only twenty minutes, but the surgery to have it reversed took four long hours under full sedation!

Later in the recovery room, he awoke with me at his side. He looked around, bewildered.

"You did it, babe!" I said, kissing him on the forehead. "Doctor says everything went well."

He looked at me with anesthesia-blurred eyes. "Babe!" he said, raising a wobbly fist to the air, "I'm one hunnit percent!"

At which point I began videotaping with my phone because let's be honest, that loopy, drugged-up, post-surgery banter is hilarious.

The hospital was great, and his nurse, Brian, took awesome care of him in the recovery room. Pretty sure loopy Dino was hitting on him for a good ten minutes before I finally stepped in to rescue the guy. "Dino, babe, you're married to me, over here. I know you're grateful to Brian, but let's leave the nice man alone."

After a few short weeks of lying low, Dino felt fully recovered and was given the all clear by his doctor. He was ready for action.

"Let's get this baby show on the road!" he told me.

And so we did.

the waiting game

A solid two months into trying for baby number four, though, and we'd seen no results. *How was that even possible?* JK! We knew this could take a while, and there was no guarantee it would work.

We had such a peace about the whole process. Statistically, reversed-vasectomy pregnancy success rates range anywhere from 30 to 90 percent. We really didn't want to push for anything God didn't want for our lives. We were simply trying to follow the path we felt He placed before us. Wherever that led, we would do our best to be content.

Obviously, the thought that we could get pregnant was ever-present, and we started talking about the what-ifs.

"What if we get pregnant soon? Where will the baby's room be in our little house?"

"Could we move ourselves into the guesthouse in the backyard and let the kids all live in the main house?" (Dino's brilliant idea, spoken like a true dad! Not really a possibility, or, like, you know, safe . . .)

The boys were now ten and nine, and they shared the room next to ours. Um, yeah. That was way too close. They were already asking questions like, "Why was Daddy 'crying' last night?" *Um, well . . .*

Our kids were not clueless, or at least they wouldn't be for much longer. Things would only get worse as they got older. We realized we might have outgrown our Spanish bungalow.

We weren't pushing to move. We could thrive in our 1,300-square-foot house by simply building an addition. We'd lived quite happily in 180 square feet, after all! Still, Redfin is my favorite app, and I was always peeking here and there to see if anything popped up.

I was proud of the improvements we'd made to this house, and another such challenge tempted me. I looked at a few options, but nothing really tugged at either one of us enough to make a swap.

Then in early February 2020, right in the midst of a normal morning—kids at school, Dino at the gym, and me running errands—I got a call from Dino: "Hey, babe, I'm at the gym with Nick. He just texted you a listing, and I think you should go look at it with him today. Like, now."

First off, that's just straight dirty talk to me. Nothing gets me more hot-and-bothered than Dino talking house stuff.

Second, who's Nick, you might ask? Nick was a young friend of ours from the gym. He and his brother, Brandon, are Realtors—young and real go-getters.

"Nick says that when they saw this house, it screamed Petrone to them," Dino said.

"Yesss!" I practically shouted back. "I'll go meet him, like, now? Or maybe, like, five minutes ago? Let's do this!" I don't hide excitement well.

An hour later, I met Nick at the address he'd texted me. As I pulled down the long, sloping driveway, a sprawling ranch house came into view. It was run down and dated, but it sat on a two-and-a-half-acre plot of land that was quiet, rustic, and majestic. I instantly called my husband.

"Dino, you need to come right now. I haven't even gone inside, but I think we should walk this place together."

"On my way," he replied. He was at the office, just twenty minutes up the freeway.

I was so tempted to go inside while I waited for Dino, but I just knew we needed to see this place together for the first time.

He pulled up and parked next to me. As he stepped out of his Jeep and looked around, I recognized the big eyes and smirky grin I knew so well. It was the expression he always had when we saw a home we'd eventually buy.

Let me paint a picture of this property: It sat at the end of a rural street, surrounded by forest and behind an electronic gate, which are all rad things. But the house itself was a dumpster fire. Let's just say it had taken a ride on the Hot-Mess Express and needed a whole lotta TLC.

Before even walking inside the house, I could see the major potential of this property, and my heart raced as I considered everything I would want to do with it. A list began forming in my mind: new exterior paint, new light fixtures, and new landscaping, for starters. The yard was so overgrown with blackberry bushes and weeds that we could barely see what was once a lawn. Clearly, no one had lived here for years.

We walked around to the back of the house. The backyard held a run-down chicken shed that looked extremely questionable. Who knew what was inside of said shed? Not chickens—at least not live chickens, that's for sure. There was also a "she shed" with a caved-in roof as well as a noticeably cracked pool that was filled with murky water and debris.

But beyond the blackberry bushes, crazy sheds, and dilapidated pool, if Dino and I stood on our tippy-toes just right, we could see a glorious, overgrown vineyard at the back side of the property. Dino squeezed my hand as we both recalled our night at Sophie James. *How cool would it be to live at a vineyard?* I'd once dreamed. Beyond the vineyard, a sweet meadow lay nestled at the foot of the redwood forest.

"Wow." We both stood there in awe, staring.

We hadn't even been inside yet, and we were already sold.

A quick tour of the house itself left us with the same feeling. It had a generous, open layout, four good-sized bedrooms, an office, and vaulted wood ceilings. Some of the rooms smelled like cat pee, and one of the bathrooms was rotting with mold. There was mouse poop everywhere. But we could see past all of that. The house had good bones. My brain was going crazy with ideas, and so was Dino's.

"We want to make an offer," Dino told Nick, without needing to say a word to me. This felt so right. We both knew it.

The only problem was that the property was out of our price range. It was more than we could probably get for our current house in town, with nothing left over for a much-needed total remodel. But we wanted to at least try for it.

D My college degree was in finance, which helped in situations like this. I started running the numbers on the sale of our current house and the purchase of this one. It was basically going to be impossible. The only chance we had of buying this property—and it was a really small chance—would be if three things fell into place:

1. We sold our Spanish house for top of market.

2. We didn't get into a crazy bidding war on the new house (which almost always happens in California because the housing market is so competitive).

3. The new house appraised as high as our offer.

If all three of these things aligned, we might just sneak in and be able to grab this place. We would then need to take our time over the next few years with the remodel as we got our finances back in order from the purchase.

Ash and I had learned the hard way that the best approach to take when making a big decision—whether it was adding a new baby to the family or buying a new home—was to seek whatever God wanted for us and not force things ourselves. This posture worked for us. It brought us peace. The way we look at it, our current house was not really ours; the new house was not ours; none of it was ours. God had loaned all of this to us for a period of time on this earth. We just wanted to be wise and honor Him with it.

After the kids were tucked in for the night, Ash and I sat down at the kitchen table. I showed her the numbers.

"It'll be a tight fit, financially," she said.

"Yep."

"I sense we should go for it, though."

"Me too. Let's pray about it." So we prayed.

"Okay, God," I said, "we really don't want to be making decisions outside of what You want for our lives, and we really don't want this house if this isn't the path that will best honor You. Our lives are Yours. Show us what You want. We'll head down this path until You make it clear that we should stop. Let's see what You're going to do!"

Then I started to hustle. Time to make some phone calls and see if there was any possibility of making this work financially. By the end of the day, I was confident in the number we could afford to offer for the new house. Not a penny more. We met up with Nick and signed offer papers.

Dino called our lender that day and got us preapproved for a loan. And we immediately listed our bungalow. The numbers between the two homes didn't quite match up. This was going to be a stretch, if it was even possible. We didn't need the bigger house to be happy, and we didn't need it to have another baby, which made it easier to keep a loose grip on our (very strong) desire to make this property our next home.

We've always felt that when we pray about something we're aligned on, we go forward as long as the doors keep opening. We trusted that if this wasn't what God wanted for us, He'd simply close the doors.

The doors kept opening.

Our Spanish bungalow officially went on the market on a Tuesday at 12:30 p.m. We listed it slightly lower than market value, hoping we'd get a few interested buyers and maybe even a bidding war. By 2:30 p.m. that day, I got a call from Nick.

"Ashley! Brandon and I want to meet you and Dino at your home at 3:30."

"All right . . . is everything okay?" I asked.

"Just meet us," he said.

Oh boy. Had the inspection uncovered a mold issue? Did the house have radon gas? But I had a hunch it was good news. Was there an offer on the table? The house had only been on the market for two hours. Surely, there wasn't a potential buyer this soon.

I called Dino and he came straight home.

"I talked to Nick on the way here," he said as he walked in, "but he wouldn't tell me a thing. You?"

"No. Nothing. He just said to meet them here."

We waited. Finally, Brandon and Nick walked up our sidewalk, looking all dapper in their suits. We sat down at our dining room table. The brothers had half grins on their faces as Nick pulled a real-estate contract out of his jacket pocket and laid it on the table, facedown.

"Do you trust us?" he asked, trying not to smile.

"Yeah, Nicky! What's up?" Dino responded.

"I have an offer for you, but I want you to sign the papers before you even see it."

What?

By the look on their faces and the intense restraint they were exercising, we knew it had to be a solid offer.

Dino looked over at me with raised eyebrows and a grin. "Yeah?" he asked.

And I nodded yes.

"Okay, Nicky, we trust you. Let's do it!"

We signed the paper and handed it back to him. He then pulled out another paper, sliding it across the table dramatically, like in a scene from a movie. "And here's the offer."

D We were 99 percent sure our offer on the new house would be accepted by the sellers, but I was stressing pretty hard with all the financial variables on our end. We absolutely needed our current home to go for top dollar. Anything less and the whole deal would collapse. Plus, we'd end up without a dime of extra cash and a house that needed a ton of work—and I mean a ton. It would take us years to save for all the projects that lay ahead. Also, the new place had to appraise for the amount we'd offered, or we'd be responsible for paying the difference out of pocket.

We were stepping out in faith, praying that God would keep this from falling through. We had done this same thing with the land in Southern California, and we knew God had been faithful even when things didn't go as we'd planned.

This felt different. It was more black-and-white. There was absolutely no wiggle room, or the numbers wouldn't work and we couldn't afford the house. No margin of error. Everything had to fit together perfectly, like pieces in a jigsaw puzzle, or we'd take it as a sign that God had closed the door.

Dino and I sat there, staring at the contract Nick had just turned over and the number he was pointing to. The offer was way more than our asking price.

Am I reading this correctly? I scanned the document, looking for something a little closer to—or even in the same ballpark as—our listing price. But the number Nick pointed to was in fact the offer. It was an out-of-this-world, only-happens-in-the-movies kind of number. This was the offer we'd just blindly signed. We'd sold our little Spanish bungalow for way more money than we ever could have dreamed.

It felt like a mic drop from God, as if He were saying, *Yeah, I'm not only going to sell your house and make this new property happen, but I'm doing so much that you'll know it's from Me. It's not just luck. It's not just the crazy California housing market. This, My sweet children, is from Me. Thanks for your willingness to surrender your desires and seek after My plan. Well, here's a gift from Me to you. Use it to buy this property—oh, and you'll have enough left over to remodel this house and make it your home.*

D Ash and I were both humbled by how this was all unfolding. Life doesn't always work out this way, as we'd learned over the years. I had spent so much time over the past years lamenting certain decisions we'd made. Each unchosen option had the potential to take us down a different path, and I wondered where those paths might have led. Should I have taken that first Netflix job? Should we have wasted all that time and money on land and dirt? Should we have moved to NorCal? Had we been too impulsive in buying our 1,300-square-foot bungalow, only to possibly lose money on a hasty sale?

All those what-ifs were eating away at me as I sat at the table. But when Nick turned over that paper and we saw the number on the document, all my concerns and uncertainty melted away. It was as if God whispered in my ear and said, *Dino, you have been on the exact path I've wanted for you the entire time. You've had a heart that desires to follow Me, and for being faithful with the little I've given you, I'm going to trust you with a little more.* Or a lot more! Now, more than anything, we wanted to honor God with this new place we'd call home.

It was clear from the sale price of our Spanish bungalow that God was paving the way for us to buy this new house—and preparing us for the next season of our lives. What amazing things did He have in store?

A week later, our offer on the house with the overgrown vineyard was accepted, and three weeks after that, we drove away from our Spanish bungalow—and all of our furniture and household items. The new owners wanted everything in our home, right down to our dishes! Given their generous offer, we were more than happy to oblige.

We had lived in that sweet Spanish bungalow for just about seventeen months—the same amount of time we'd lived in the trailer. And once again, we were driving away from our home with only our personal belongings. But we had everything we needed: our family, the prospect of a Hot-Mess Express we would get to remodel, and five extremely thankful hearts.

the hot-mess express

I don't like to waste time. Before we relocated, I'd made lists of all the things we wanted and needed to do to the house. We moved in early March, and by then I'd already contracted workers for each job.

For previous house projects, Dino and I had created a little three-list system that helped us wrap our heads around all that needed to happen with a remodel. The list included our different priorities and who was responsible for each. It was a great way for us to see clearly what we needed to do, who was going to do it, and what it was going to cost. Here's an overview of the three lists that make up our system:

1. **Immediate: Do now.** This list includes projects addressing safety issues (electrical problems, mold, or other health hazards) as well as fixing leaks, painting, and replacing flooring while the house is still empty so we don't have to move furniture twice. Because we will need at least one functioning toilet, shower, sink, fridge, and microwave once we move in, if we lack any of them, they go on the list. The kitchen in our new house needed to be completely gutted, so we added this to our "Before Move-In" list.

2. **Secondary: Do soon.** These are second-tier jobs that can be done after we've moved in. Remodeling additional baths, painting the exterior, landscaping, and stenciling went on this list for our new house.

3. **Later: Do eventually.** These are blue-sky projects. They're not essential but would sure be nice once our budget allows. Fixing our dilapidated pool and restoring the overgrown vineyard fell on this list.

I know there are apps and online programs specifically designed to plan for a remodel, but for me, a simple yellow notepad does the trick. My brain needs to see the lists laid out in this format before I feel I can successfully execute them.

We didn't hire a general contractor to oversee all the work for this home remodel, but we did hire subcontractors for the skilled projects we couldn't do

ourselves. We also hired Gerry, the handyman who had played a key role in remodeling our Spanish bungalow. Gerry is a saint and has basically become part of our family. If anything needed to be done, he could do it, and he always replied to my never-ending requests with "Sure, Ash" in his old-school New Jersey accent.

For this remodel, I was essentially the general contractor on the design projects and Dino covered all the technical and functional sides of the remodel. We've found when we allow each other to lead in our own areas of exper-tise and use our different strengths, we work very well together. Our projects are completed with less arguing and fewer bumps. Key words: *Less. Fewer.* They still happen, for sure. But we've worked really hard in our marriage to build trust and respect for each other, which just natu-rally overflow into this area as well. It creates more harmony—and way more fun—when we're working together.

When we allow each other to lead in our own areas of expertise and use our different strengths, we work very well together.

shelter in place

Gerry is accustomed to my fast pace and is just as quick as I am when it comes to jumping on a project. By the middle of March 2020, we had already ripped out our kitchen, all of the gross flooring, and most of the bathrooms. Our painters were in the midst of painting the whole house. But that day, things kind of shifted, not just for our family but for all of California. On Thursday, March 19, our governor issued a statewide shelter-in-place order due to the coronavirus pandemic. The whole nation soon followed suit.

Under this order, schools closed down and only "essential service" businesses were permitted to remain open. Dino and his staff were told to work from home, but in the construction industry—and for guys like Gerry and the crews we'd already hired—the shutdown had far-reaching effects.

Because we'd already basically demolished the inside of the house, our home was deemed unlivable. With no running water, nails coming out of the floor, mold in the kids' bathroom, and a giant hole in our bedroom wall that exposed us to the backyard, finishing the remodel fell in the category of an "essential service." We were able to keep moving forward on our project. *Phew!*

Our core work crew was basically Dino, me, the kids (now ten, nine, and six), and Gerry. At first, I was stressed about how we'd handle school—classes would be moving to an online format and our internet service was spotty at best. Our home was completely torn up so there was nowhere to set up a distraction-free study area, and given my responsibilities with the remodel, I didn't have hours each day to spend homeschooling my kids. They would have to do their online schoolwork in less-than-ideal conditions, whenever the internet was working.

Dino and I agreed to focus on what our kids could get from this unexpected global disruption rather than on what they were missing.

First, our kids had both parents home all day, every day, which gave us time to work with them on the way they related to one another. Second, they were providing practical help on our home's projects, picking up skills and life experience they would have missed out on if they had been away at school during the day. Finally, instead of reading about how people dealt with things in history books, they were learning how to deal with history in the making.

Just when I'd shifted my perspective in a healthier direction, I was reminded that home renovations never go as planned. Within that first month, everything in this house broke. *Everything.* The water heater, both air-conditioning units, both furnaces—pretty much all the expensive things. You know, the stuff that's not fun to spend money on. We had no heat, no central air, no running water, no functioning kitchen. Thankfully with the sale of our old home, we were able to absorb these unexpected costs, and the Hot-Mess Express rolled on.

Oh, and I discovered where the weird cat pee smell was coming from. It was pee all right, just not from a cat. When we first moved in, we set up our laundry room as a makeshift kitchen since we were demolishing the actual kitchen. The weird smell was definitely strongest in the laundry room, but we could not locate it. I about gagged when, long after we'd moved our temporary kitchen out of that room, we discovered a giant mouse nest completely filling the dryer-vent pipe that led to the outside. Right. Above. Where. I. Had. Prepared. Our. Food. Hundreds—yes, hundreds—of mice had been living there, peeing and pooping, rent-free.

The mice also loved our bedroom, and since one wall was basically just a giant hole to the backyard covered with plastic, it was hard to keep them out. One night I awoke to the sound of a little tinkering and some scratching on Dino's side of the bed. Maybe some chewing?

"Dino!" I poked him and he sat straight up, wide-awake. Neither of us were sleeping too soundly in this dumpster fire of a house. He grabbed his phone and turned on its flashlight.

Scanning the room with his phone, the light landed on the nightstand right next to his head. A mouse sat contentedly on a plate, eating the remains of Dino's late-night snack.

"Nooo!" he yelled.

I dove under the covers as the mouse scurried off into our bathroom.

"That's it. We need to move," Dino joked.

Neither of us slept that night, and on my yellow notepad the next morning, I bumped "GET RID OF MICE!" to the top of my "Immediate" list.

design with intention

This house was definitely large and in charge. So much to be done—and I wanted it all done now. Although it was more square footage than we needed, I knew we were here for a purpose, and we wanted to be generous with our space. I thought of Jesus' words in Luke: "From the one who has been entrusted with much, much more will be asked."[10] God had entrusted this abundance to us, and I wanted to make sure we were using every bit of space wisely. My vision was simple. I wanted

God had entrusted this abundance to us, and I wanted to make sure we were using every bit of space wisely.

to design a home for people, not things—a safe, inviting space for new friends and old alike, a place where our kids and our marriage would thrive and where rich friendships would grow.

My goal in every remodel decision was to make this space cozy, incorporate elements to meet the needs of our family, and not fill it with a bunch of stuff.

I also had the thought of a little new babe in the back of my mind. We had been trying to get pregnant for a few months now, and I knew the statistics. Chances were slim, and it could take years if it were to happen at all.

But I didn't want to think that way. I wanted to think rationally, but I also wanted to think with a thankful and faithful spirit. God had brought us here to this crazy house, for who knows what? He had not guaranteed us another baby, but it felt right to incorporate the thought of an added Petrone into our home's design.

The house's architecture had a natural French château vibe, so my design choices were influenced by that feel. I've never been to Europe, let alone France, but I had some made-up ideas of exactly what that looked like. Also, Pinterest. And Instagram.

The kids' bathroom was one of the first spots I designed. It was a large open space with double vanities, nasty carpet (just like the rest of the house), and a rotted-out floor in the shower stall. Lovely. But I saw it for exactly what it was meant to be: a bathroom for four kiddos.

I found fun little bucket wall sinks, two for one side and two for the other. True, we had only three kids, but four sinks balanced out the room and just felt right.

After Gerry removed the mold from the shower area (major health hazard!) and the space was taken down to new studs, I designed the kids' shower with a simple black-and-white hexagon tile. I was searching for a word to write in the shower with those tiles. I wanted something that represented our family well, and I just kept coming back to the word *joy*. Our family's intention over these past few years had been to find joy in everything, even in a moldy bathroom.

> *Our family's intention over these past few years
> had been to find joy in everything.*

But since we were going with a French theme in the house, I picked the French word for joy, *joie*, and added three flowers, one for each kid, on one side of the shower. On the other side, I added an extra flower in the hope that a baby might one day complete this bathroom designed for four.

I covered lots of walls in other rooms with either board-and-batten or shiplap to make each room cozier. Other features—hardware, light fixtures, color palettes—were influenced purely by what we loved.

One of my favorite finds was our porcelain kitchen counters in a cookies-and-cream coloring—they look like solid marble and are super dramatic. I loved them so much that we also used them as our backsplash and even framed one of our fireplaces with it. It was an unexpected pick, but it was perfect for this home.

finding *joie* in the in-between

This was by far the biggest project Dino and I had worked on together. There were so many projects to juggle and so many decisions to be made. It didn't come without stresses and complications, but we had so much fun doing it together. We trusted and respected each other's decisions in our respective areas, and yet we still leaned into one another as partners, every step of the way. I loved working with this guy. We were having way too much fun.

I also loved sharing this journey with my Instagram community. Friends tuned in daily to see what crazy thing was happening at Château Petrone. They cheered when things went well and groaned with me at every setback along the way. With the many ups and downs of this project, those friends became a constant reminder that even on a day when remodel bumps prevailed, I could still find joy in the in-between. My @arrowsandbow friends are just the best!

After living in an RV where emptying our sewage tanks every Saturday was our norm, making dinner in a rusty laundry room sink circa 1983 didn't seem so terrible. Taking cold showers until the new water heaters were installed wasn't anyone's favorite thing, but it seemed easier just to roll with it than to complain. (And yeah, maybe we just didn't take full showers for excessive amounts of time in that season. Who's to say?)

We had developed a new mindset, looking at each circumstance through a lens of thankfulness and excitement to see what God had in store for us next. And on April 4, in the midst of home remodel, mice droppings, and a pandemic, we got to see just what God had been planning all along.

planning your remodel

Starting a home remodel or even a one-room project can feel overwhelming. Before you become paralyzed with indecision, let's look at the three biggest questions I hear from my friends on Instagram: Where do I begin? Who does what? And what's the best order to proceed?

If you've asked these questions, you're not alone! On page 224, we introduced our three-list system for prioritizing projects at the start of a home renovation. Here are some additional tips to get your project underway, keep it manageable, and make sure it stays on track.

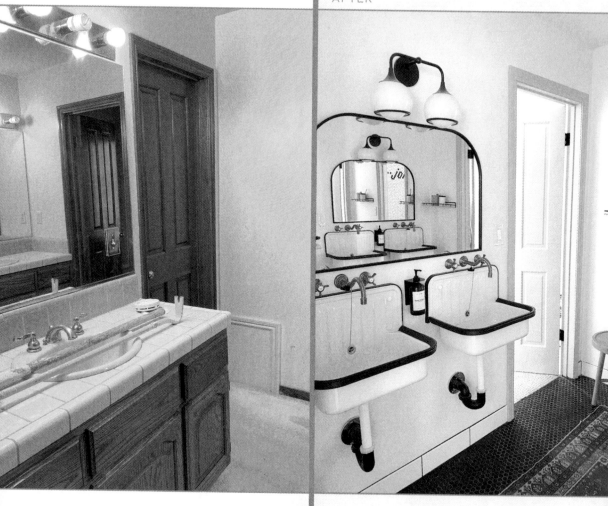

QUICK TIPS

▶ Make a list that organizes projects by priority: Immediate, Secondary, and Later.

▶ Prioritize safety and structural issues.

▶ Think DIY: What projects that don't require a licensed technician could you do yourself?

PLANNING YOUR REMODEL

>>> **Make your list.** There is no right or wrong way to make your list. If you're tech savvy, you can create a list using an app or even the notes feature on your phone. Or if you're old school like me and love the satisfaction of making check marks or crossing off items on a list, a simple pad of paper works great.

Once you've chosen whatever method comes naturally to you, break up your project list into three parts: Immediate, Secondary, and Later. This will help you see clearly what needs to happen first. I like to create three side-by-side columns for this part. That way if I decide something has changed in priority, it's easy to move it from one column to the next.

• **First things first: safety and struc-ture.** Ideally, work like taking out walls, gutting a kitchen, or replac-ing flooring should be done before moving in. Ditto with addressing safety issues by updating question-able wiring, removing mold, or repairing gas lines in need of repair. Think through the engineering of your house: plumbing, electrical, and HVAC systems. Those projects come before the fun stuff like room decor.

• **First things second: walls and flooring.** After any safety issues have been addressed and before you haul in the moving boxes and furniture, consider addressing your new home's "canvas"—namely the walls and flooring that will set off your decor. I like to paint walls before putting in new floors or carpeting so I don't need to worry too much about splatter. Next, I tackle flooring. If you're in a time crunch, think about what you can do quickly without having to move furniture twice. It's not the end of the world if you need to paint or refloor after move-in, but it's definitely easier to do it beforehand.

>>> **Think DIY: What can you do yourself?** Do-it-yourself (DIY) projects can feel intimidating, but I promise, they're fun and oh-so-satisfying. They can also save you lots of dollars. Painting is one of my favorite DIYs because the equipment is an affordable, one-time purchase; the skills are easy to learn; and it makes such a quick difference. Along with instant gratification, it allows you to express your creativity with the peace of mind in knowing you can easily cover up mistakes.

⟫ Why Take Out a Wall? ⟪

One of my favorite big projects is to take out a wall that serves no purpose. Here's what you need to know for this rewarding little gem of a project:

1. **Ask what you'll gain.** Will it open up the kitchen into the living space? Get rid of a hallway you don't need? Bring natural light into a dim room? Merge two small living spaces or bedrooms into one big one? Can you enfold that formal dining room into an open kitchen? All are great reasons to consider removing a wall.

2. **Ask what you'll lose.** Maybe you don't need that extra bedroom now, but will you need it in three years? Would removing a wall mean that your bedroom or a bathroom would open directly into the living room? Would removing the wall make the house too noisy? Would the flooring repair make the project too costly? Weigh the gains and losses before deciding.

3. **Hire it out.** If you decide you want to take out the wall, plan to bring in a professional. Taking down a wall isn't a DIY project because walls often hide things like air vents and electrical wires. Also, that wall might be weight bearing, and it's not a great idea to remove something that's holding up your roof! Get opinions and estimates from licensed professionals, then choose someone you trust and can afford.

Removing a wall almost always makes it easier for our family to be relational, whether it's just us or we're entertaining guests. We're not really formal people, so creating one open space from two smaller ones (such as formal dining and living rooms) whenever possible makes sense. Do what works best for your family.

Most do-it-yourselfers aren't highly trained geniuses who went to design school. They're people like you and me who were curious enough to try something new. Here's a list of DIY projects that can make a huge difference in your home—and are easy to learn:

- paint interior
- paint or stain exterior
- stencil old tile or flooring to make it look new or updated
- replace dated cabinet hardware
- hang wallpaper
- add shiplap or board-and-batten siding to your walls
- reface your kitchen cabinets
- replace outdated doorknobs
- paint or refinish your home's front door
- landscape your yard
- install new flooring
- install pantry or closet shelving
- refinish furniture
- paint the trim around doors to give your hallway a little update
- hang a gallery of photos with matching frames on a blank wall
- make a small above-ground swimming pool from a galvanized metal stock tank, available at most home-supply or farm stores. Hang a filter and water pump on the side to keep it clean and fresh.
- build a cornhole game for your family to enjoy

If you're not sure how to do something—whether it's painting, installing shiplap, refinishing cabinets, or putting up wallpaper—YouTube is your BFF. The sheer number of how-to tutorials is mind-blowing. You can learn just about anything you need to know. Or search Instagram for a home blogger like me who offers how-to steps and photos.

Some things like plumbing and electrical just won't be feasible to do yourself because they're dangerous and require a licensed professional, but for other jobs, I challenge you to get out of your comfort zone and tackle those doable tasks on your remodel list. It'll save you loads of money, and you'll feel satisfaction in designing a cozy home with your own hands.

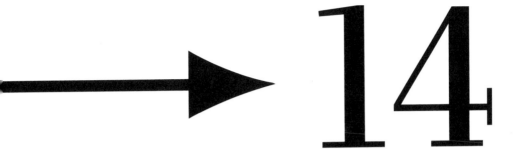

14

living by design

"Good morning, babe," I said to Dino. "Do you want a side of baby with your coffee?"

Let me back up.

My period wasn't due for a few days, but I just had a feeling. . . . I'd gotten up early that cold April morning and tiptoed out of our bedroom so as not to wake Dino. I ran across the hall into the kids' bathroom—currently the only one working in the Hot-Mess Express. And I took a pregnancy test.

I sat there waiting for the three full minutes per the instructions on the box. Then I peeked. A faint but definite blue line was coming into focus on the white stick.

"No way!" I whispered out loud in the bathroom to absolutely no one. My hands started shaking. This was happening!

I know some women who wait until a special dinner out or a big occasion to share their pregnancy news with the baby's dad. But I'm not exactly one to wait, and I suck at keeping secrets. Dino would be able to read it all over my face as soon as he saw me, so I quickly started some coffee and then hopped back into bed. I couldn't even stand waiting any longer or think of anything more clever to say, so I just blurted out, "Do you want a side of baby with your coffee?" Whatever that means—LOL! But he knew instantly what I was saying.

"Are you really pregnant? Are you serious?" he asked.

I nodded.

"Shut your mouth!" he said, grinning.

"I'm shaking right now," I said, laughing.

"Baby! Baby," he said, rolling toward me and kissing me.

It had happened. We were expecting another baby.

The kids were thrilled to hear the news that another Petrone was on its way. We announced our good news immediately to everyone. I mean everyone—family, friends, and all of our followers on Instagram. Of course, another miscarriage was a possibility. Those feelings of worry rush right in without permission, especially when you've experienced a pregnancy loss before. But I was just so excited that we could even get pregnant after Dino's surgery that I didn't want to think that way. Only positive thoughts!

Selling one house, buying another, moving, remodeling the new home—and sure, let's throw a post-vasectomy baby into the mix! Why not? Bring it, 2020.

Ash and I have very similar mindsets when it comes to tackling new challenges. We beast through. This next season was going to be a bit harder than usual, though, since the remodel was far from done, and Ash gets super sick when she's pregnant. She's our general contractor for home remodels, and the pregnancy meant I would be losing my teammate until she got through the worst of the morning sickness. So be it! Small price to pay in exchange for rounding out the Petrone team with a grand finale.

"Ugh, Dino. Please stop smoking meat!"

I got hit with morning sickness right on the dot at six weeks pregnant. Suddenly I was dashing my husband's dreams of smoking meat and planning delicious food because all I wanted to eat was whatever would not make me puke at any given moment.

Morning sickness is not ideal during a home remodel. I felt so gross, and I completely lost the ability to make decisions.

"What's that, Quinn? You wanna add kitty-pattern curtains to your bedroom? Sure. That's fine . . . whatever you want. Just don't ask me any more questions, mmk?"

Luckily, we had worked so rapidly during the first two months that most of the major decisions had already been made. So I only needed to do some light brain work and power through.

I was so exhausted, I felt drugged. But Gerry was retiling our master bathroom at the time, so naps in our bedroom weren't an option. Also, we didn't have a sofa yet, so I couldn't nap in the living room either. Thankfully my mom is a saint. She drove up and took over the DIY jobs I had been working on, thus making the sickness so much more bearable.

Dino also played a huge role. He went out of his way to help me through my morning sickness. He was even quicker than usual to respond to the kids' needs so I didn't have to, and if he was home when I lost my lunch (or breakfast or dinner) in the toilet, he'd often hold back my hair or offer me a cold washcloth. I was pretty miserable and grumpy, but he was just so loving and tender toward me, no matter how un-fun I was to be around.

During my pregnancies with the first three kiddos, I don't ever remember him serving me while I was sick without grumbling or making me feel as if he was just checking a box. We were so much younger, and neither of us had worked through our own demons and the major hurdles we still needed to face in our marriage. So there was that.

This was the first time I actually felt as if Dino and I were doing a pregnancy together. I felt so loved that it gave me more energy. Despite the morning sickness and exhaustion of early pregnancy, I still had a desire to love and serve him, and to be with him physically. It was the upward spiral at work! His thoughts, words, and actions toward me made me feel so great that I wanted him to feel the same way.

 I thought back often to the drive into work when I had visualized the two paths at a fork in the road while we were praying about the idea of having another baby. I knew the path I had chosen. I had chosen the road of sacrifice, knowing it would require me to be stretched. I wanted to lean into that as much as possible. During Ash's previous three pregnancies, I hadn't been the man I wished I had been. I viewed her morning sickness as her problem, and I left her to deal with it on her own without lightening her load by increasing my share of the responsibilities with the kids. *Ugh.* Now I'd been given another opportunity to do it over. To do it right.

blindfolds and chalk paint

By now you know that we like to move fast. If we have the option of not waiting, we will surely take that route! We wanted to know the sex of this baby, and technology is so advanced that I was able get my blood drawn at just eleven weeks—and the lab promised to text us the results only seven days later.

Quinn wanted to know if this baby would be a brother or a sister. She'd been praying every night for months that God would give her a sister. We'd gently encouraged her to pray for a healthy baby and told her that God would help her be happy no matter which sex the baby was. But still. C'mon. The girl wanted a sister!

I didn't care whether it was a girl or a boy. I just wanted a healthy babe, and I was still so excited that we could get pregnant at all.

We had invited Greg and Hillary over for dinner, and I was in town picking up groceries when the text from my doctor arrived. I was so excited, but I didn't open it. I wanted to surprise Dino, myself, and the kids all at the same time. I had a plan.

I swung by the craft store and picked up two cans of washable spray chalk—a blue can and a pink can. Once home, I explained my plan to Dino, who grinned and set about collecting one more prop: a blindfold.

When Greg and Hillary arrived that afternoon, the kids and I dragged them from their car into the backyard, very excited.

"Wanna help us reveal the sex of our baby?" I asked, handing Hillary my phone.

"Um, yes, please!" she replied, still confused.

Dino was waiting in the backyard with our props: a blindfold long enough to wrap around both our heads and the two cans of chalk paint.

"Okay, here's how it's going down, people," I explained. "Greg, you and Hillary are gonna blindfold Dino and me back-to-back, and then you'll open the text from my doctor's office to see if it's a boy or a girl."

"What's with the spray paint?" Greg asked.

"Chalk paint," I said. "Washable. Whichever sex the baby is, you spray us with that color paint—pink for a girl, blue for a boy. Then we can take off the blindfold. Got it?"

"Got it!" they said in unison.

Gabe, Gavin, and Quinn crowded around, excited.

"Um, nope! All kids inside," Dino said. "Otherwise, you three will give it away as soon as you see the paint can. Watch from the window and come out as soon as we take off our blindfolds. Gabe, you're in charge of keeping everyone inside until then."

"Got it!" he said, and they raced into the house. Their three faces were soon mashed against the window, watching as Greg blindfolded us, back-to-back.

"Okay, can you see anything?" he asked.

"Nope!" I said.

"Not a thing!" Dino said.

"All right, we're opening the text . . . ," Greg said.

Then a moment of silence.

Agh! I was so nervous. I didn't give a care about the sex, truly. Quinn obviously wanted a sister, and Dino was also hoping for a girl. But in the end a healthy baby was all that mattered.

"Wow!" Hillary said. "I mean, just . . . wow!" I heard her shaking one of the paint cans, then felt the cold spray of the chalk as she circled around us. Then the spraying stopped.

"Okay, babe, you ready?" Dino asked.

"No. I'm so scared! I don't know why," I said.

"Well, let's go," he said.

We ripped the blindfold off and I looked down. My front was covered with a fine layer of pink chalk.

"Woohoo! It's a girl!" I said, turning to face Dino.

"Ah! Hahaha! I knew it! I knew it!" he screamed. Hugging me, he turned toward the house and shouted to Quinn, "Baby girl! We got another girl!"

The three kids came tearing out of the house, Quinn in the lead. She leapt into her daddy's arms, squeezing him tight around the neck. The boys wrapped me in their arms, and soon the five of us were a mass of hugs, laughter, and pink chalk.

How many nights had this girl prayed for a baby sister? And here we were, a year later, celebrating a baby girl in Mama's belly.

"God knew I wanted a sister," Quinn said.

"He knew," I said.

D What a journey it had been. I had leaned into this whole baby thing in faith, that whatever God wanted for us, I would be down for it. He had put a daughter on my heart and given us the name Fox (or Foxi for a girl) before we had even decided to get the reversal.

When we took our blindfold off that afternoon, I heard Ash yell, "It's a girl!" and my heart exploded. All I could think about was Quinn. I will never forget that moment when she leapt into my arms, the moment God gave the gift of a baby girl to me and my daughter.

déjà vu

At around seventeen weeks, I saw a light at the end of the morning-sickness tunnel. Suddenly, the meat Dino was constantly smoking or grilling didn't smell so bad, and the residual smoke smell that clung to him wasn't as repulsive either.

"Yay! I'm getting my taste buds back!" I announced at dinner. "I'm starting to feel like me again!"

This was such an odd time in history to be pregnant. Because of medical restrictions due to the COVID-19 pandemic, doctor's offices were allowing only patients, not their families, through the doors. Dino drove me to my doctor's appointments but then had to sit in the car and wait for me to come out. I was bummed that I had to solo my appointments, but my mind had been so preoccupied with morning sickness that the appointments had been a nice distraction.

My twenty-week 3D ultrasound appointment crept up fast. I couldn't wait to see our little angel baby's face! I drove myself so Dino could stay home. His parents were in town, and his mom, Connie, offered to go with me while Dean and Dino hung out so we ladies could dominate a day of shopping afterward.

"You don't mind waiting in the car, Con?" I asked her as we pulled into the clinic parking lot. "It should only be like thirty minutes, tops."

"Not at all, honey," she said. "I'll get some work done on my phone. See you in a few."

I walked into the building excited for this quickie ultrasound. It was the fun one where they measure you and you get to see all the cute shots of your baby.

Our ultrasound tech, Deb, met me in the exam room. "This is just a routine exam," she said. "We'll be checking the baby's heart and your placenta. Shouldn't take too long. If I see anything unusual, I'll grab your doctor to take a look."

The images on the screen were so clear. I could see baby Foxi's hands, arms, feet, and even her tiny face! But Deb kept taking more and more stills. My half-hour appointment dragged into an hour, with Deb capturing all kinds of shots from different angles. She grew very quiet. My heart began to race. *What is she seeing? What's wrong?*

"Let me go grab the doctor," she said, and left the room. My eyes filled with tears. *Not again. Please, Lord, not again.*

As soon as the doctor walked in with Deb, I asked him, "Is something wrong?"

"We're going to take some more images," he said. "We noticed some issues with her heart and the placenta."

I lay down and the doctor squirted more lubricant onto my already lubed belly.

Another hour passed as he worked. I just lay there, alone, tears streaming down my face. When he was through, the doctor said a bunch of stuff I just didn't understand. All I heard was, "There's a problem with her heart and the blood flow, and her placenta is oddly formed. It might cause her to grow incorrectly."

What he told me next made me go numb: Though he assured me that the baby's issues might resolve on their own, he referred me to a neonatal cardiologist and also suggested I set up an appointment with a genetic counselor to discuss my options, just in case I wanted to consider terminating the pregnancy.

I was sick to my stomach. "I'm sorry, what?" I asked. "What did you say? Can I please FaceTime with my husband so he can hear all this?" All I wanted to do was call Dino and sob.

"I'm sorry, no," the doctor said. "The hospital doesn't permit video."

"Could I at least record what you're explaining so he can hear it for himself when I get home?"

"That's against hospital policy," he said. "He can call me. Just come back in three weeks, and we'll check everything again. Like I said, sometimes these things work themselves out."

And with that, I got dressed and left the office.

> **D** The last time Ash had gone to a doctor's appointment alone, she had called me sobbing with news of the miscarriage. I've never forgotten that feeling of waiting to hear from her—and wondering.
>
> With this pregnancy, every visit to the doctor had been torture while I waited in the car for a call or text saying everything was fine. It had been a couple of hours since Ash and my mom left for the appointment, and we'd heard nothing. I began to get nervous. She should have called by now. What was going on? I'd been texting like crazy but was getting nothing but radio silence.

I held it together until I got outside, and then I burst into tears. Connie got out of the car and hugged me as I tried to explain.

"Let me drive you home," she said. "You call Dino. He's been texting."

I could barely communicate to poor Dino over the phone what the doctor had said and what I was feeling.

> **D** "Something is wrong . . . her heart . . . and her placenta," Ash told me through her tears.
>
> We'd been down this path before. *No! It can't be. This makes no sense!* God wouldn't let this happen to us, right? We'd prayed about this. We'd sensed God wanting us to try to get pregnant—and we'd obeyed each step of the way. And then to end up with issues? No way. No. Way. *It has to end well. It has to!*
>
> I got off the phone and walked back to our bedroom, where I broke down. I just slumped onto the floor and began weeping. I'd been on the ground crying like this once before—eight years ago after Ash called from the doctor's office with news that there was no heartbeat. This time, as I sat crying, I asked God for perspective on all of this. I needed to see what He was seeing through this situation. I needed to verbally process so I could get my thoughts out, but Ash wasn't home to hear them. Instead, I opened up a journal and began to write. This is what came out:

I'm mentally struggling with how to handle the news that Foxi might have a heart condition. I had expectations. I expected that every-thing would go perfectly, and Foxi would come out happy and healthy. That's natural, and it just takes a minute to reset to a new set of expectations.

But that's not the main issue I'm struggling with. My struggle is with how to posture myself. When I look at the men of God in Scripture, their faith was so impressive. I can imagine them in my position, and no doubt they would declare in faith, "Foxi will be fine! I trust in God, and I have faith that God will heal my daughter."

But I am torn because my prayer from the start has been, "For Your glory, Father . . . whatever You have planned for our lives, what-ever You have planned for Foxi, good or bad, my heart's desire is for it all to honor You."

Which brings me to my struggle. How do I reconcile the belief that God can make Foxi healthy with my desire to dedicate myself and my family to Him—good or bad? Which does not always mean good things will happen.

In the bedroom as I waited for Ash and Mom to get home, I felt as if God was pulling me into a different mindset. Whatever was to happen with Foxi, I wanted to live my faith boldly. No matter what happened, God, without a doubt, could bring good from this situation. We live in a fallen world, where imperfection and heartbreak exist. But every situation can be faced and lived out in a way that honors Him.

I closed my journal, feeling at peace about whatever we were facing with

> *We live in a fallen world, where imperfection and heartbreak exist. But every situation can be faced and lived out in a way that honors God.*

Foxi. I would ask God to make her healthy and whole. And I'd accept what-ever happened. As I had told Quinn months ago at bedtime, God doesn't always say yes to our prayers. Sometimes He says no. But as we pray, He changes our hearts.

I couldn't fix our circumstances, but I could choose my outlook. I fully believe we're put on this earth to make the most of the lives God has given us. No matter what happens, good or bad, I want to honor Him.

I couldn't believe this was happening again. During the first few weeks of this pregnancy, I had moments or even random days when I would wonder, *What if something happens?* But Dino kept reminding me not to dwell on those thoughts, to bring those anxieties to God and shift my mindset from fear to thankfulness.

So I did just that. Whenever I worried, I prayed, *For Your glory, God. Whatever is to happen, may it honor You.*

As Connie drove me home, I remembered those prayers. *Whatever is to happen...*

The gift of being pregnant with this baby girl was just that—a gift. I remem-bered how we had done our best to seek God's guidance, then got a vasectomy reversal, found a home to fit a family of six, and then waited on whatever God had planned. Each of these memories brought comfort.

Back at the house, Dino met me at the door and wrapped his arms around me. Connie and Dean took the kids out back because we didn't want to bring them into this news just yet. We had three weeks until the next appointment when we'd learn more.

As Dino and I talked and cried, we were shocked to discover how similarly we were approaching this. During my short drive home, I'd landed at the same conclu-sion he had.

"Let's honor God with our lives and Foxi's, no matter where this leads, babe," I said.

"Absolutely. That's the plan," Dino said. "We got this. God's got us."

I shared what was going on with Foxi on Instagram. The messages of prayer and support from this community were overwhelming. The comfort of knowing others were praying for her—people I'd never even met—upheld me during those weeks.

I was just so thankful for however God would use us and our baby. It truly brought me so much peace.

The next three weeks weren't as torturous as I'd expected. They were more like an in-between, filled with waiting, finding joy even amid the unknown.

When the day of the next appointment finally arrived, Dino insisted on driving.

"Yeah, no more missing appointments for me, thank you very much," he said. "My heart can't take it! I'll just sit here solo in the car."

Once inside, I lay back on the ultrasound table, knowing what to expect this time. I felt at peace, and my mind was fully engaged, rather than shut down with shock. I sort of remembered what her heart had looked like on the earlier images, and I was eager and prepared to ask questions this time.

I didn't wait for the doctor to report what he saw. "How's the placenta?" I asked.

"It looks great, actually," he said. "She's growing, and there are no abnormalities to it whatsoever."

Phew! Check! One concern down, one to go.

Before I could even ask about Foxi's heart, the doctor spoke up.

"Deb," he said to the tech, "look at her heart. These scans are beautiful. We need to share them in our next department meeting." Then turning to me, he asked, "All right with you, Ashley?"

I tried to take it all in. "Sure. Um, so, her heart looks . . . good?"

"Her heart looks great. The blood is flowing nicely, and everything seems to have resolved itself perfectly."

The next three weeks were like an in-between, filled with waiting, finding joy even amid the unknown.

Now I was crying again. *I guess that's just what I do in this room*, I thought. But it seemed so fitting, and frankly, I didn't care as the tears of joy and excitement flowed. *Thank You, God.*

I ran out of that office as fast as a pregnant lady could and jumped into Dino's waiting arms. Poor guy had been pacing back and forth outside—I'm sure in mental anguish—dying to know what was going on inside.

"She's fine! Everything's fine!" I blurted out between blubbery tears. Dino wanted details.

"Heart?" he asked.

"Fine! In fact, 'beautiful,' according to the doctor!"

"Placenta?"

"Also fine! Perfectly normal!"

Our little miracle baby was just that, a sweet miracle. We would have loved her no matter what, of course. But hearing she was healthy with no abnormalities—it's what every parent dreams. We climbed into the car and just sat there saying, "Thank You, God! Thank You, God!"

Dino added, "Now help her parents honor You with how we live our lives."

prelude

The remodel of Château Petrone was wrapping up nicely. With 95 percent of the interior work done, we were now just sitting and waiting for our baby girl to arrive.

Things in our life were slowing down, largely because the country was still shut down due to the pandemic. Schools were still teaching kids online; Dino was still working from home; and restaurants, movie theaters, beaches, and parks were closed. There weren't many places to go.

For the first time ever, we were okay with a season of slow. We were hunkered down like the rest of the country, and it felt good to rest. Okay, well, our version of rest might be a little different from others'. We still had all the outside land-scaping to do, a pool to repair, and a vineyard to restore, all while planning for a baby—oh, and now I was writing a book. But this was just us thriving in orga-nized chaos.

Even so, I began slowing down a few months before Foxi's birth. My body was basically screaming at me to stop all the madness. Between the backache, joint pain, and pelvic pain, it was clearly telling me it had had just about enough of me lugging this giant watermelon around inside.

Yet I experienced what I call random acts of nesting, too, like the Sunday before church when I got a sudden urge to clear leaves and debris from our extremely long, steep driveway with our heavy blower. Always a good idea in the third trimester!

Dino watched me, cracking up. "Wouldn't you like the boys to do that, Ash?"

"Nope! I'm good!" I hollered back. For some reason, I just really needed to clear that driveway myself.

I soaked it all in, treasuring those days. I figured this was my last baby, which gave me a fresh perspective. Every ache and pain, every sleepless night, every kick from Foxi was a gift. My heart felt absolutely full of love for the child inside my womb. She was an incredible gift.

As the calendar days ticked by in anticipation of her arrival, my constant prayer was just three words: *Thank You, God.*

furnishing your home with intention

Once the bulk of this house's interior remodel was complete, it was time to think about furnishings. How did I want to fill this space?

Obviously, we'd been living here for several months, so we had already bought the basics like beds, dressers, and a table to eat on. As I thought about adding the missing pieces, I wanted to focus on filling our home with intention, just as I had in the trailer and our Spanish bungalow. This house was much bigger. It felt a little overwhelming. But just because I now had the space didn't mean I had to cram stuff in it. I wanted to create a space for people, not for things.

In fact, during the remodel, we'd made some big structural decisions based on our priorities of relationships, not stuff. The same principle applied to interior design. How could I make design choices for people rather than things?

BEFORE

AFTER

BEFORE

AFTER

QUICK TIPS

▶ Make the most of the flat space (walls, windows, and doors) in each room first.

▶ Design rooms that support how you actually live.
▶ Convert unused storage space into functional space.

FURNISHING YOUR HOME WITH INTENTION

If you resonate with our priorities of designing for people, not objects, here are three key principles to keep in mind.

>>> **Focus on flat space (walls, windows, and floors).** When it comes to design, we often limit our thinking to the three-dimensional stuff in a room—like sofas, side tables, and decor. All those things leave less space for people. Plus they become dated and may turn to clutter over time.

Begin by focusing on the flat space in your home. Walls, windows, ceilings, and floors take up zero space, but they can do a lot of work for you in creating the vibe you want in a room.

Could you add a contrast wall with a bold color of paint? Stencil a faux-tile backsplash? Add wood detailing (board-and-batten or ship-lap) or put up some wallpaper to make the space feel cozy? Would a colorful rug help the space feel well-designed without adding furniture that takes up space? Could you add a window or skylight to a dimly lit room? Strip those painted wood beams on your ceiling? Or hang cool window dressings to spice things up? If so, start there. Then add the 3D stuff bit by bit, once your flat space is just how you want it.

>>> **Design for how you live.** What's right for one family may not be right for another. Some people love eating dinner at a dining table every night, while others may connect better with plates on their laps around a sofa or at the island on bar stools. Where do you naturally gather? Where do your guests naturally hang out when they come over? Design toward that.

If you rarely sit down at a table to eat, don't dedicate an entire room for formal dining. Don't hog all that space with a giant table and chairs for twelve. Instead, choose a small table with pull-out leaves for when company comes over. You can use folding chairs for those rare larger gatherings, but you don't need to buy (and store) twelve dining-room chairs year-round.

Do friends and family tend to gather at your cool kitchen island? Invest in comfy chairs for that space. Do they love to eat in the family room? Swap out your coffee table for one that pops up into a table. Or swap your end tables for a set of stacking tables that also work as TV trays. Get creative and find solutions that fit how you actually live.

Sometimes we give in to outside pressures (friends, parents, Instagram, Pinterest) to do our homes a certain way. Don't even go there. Remember, there is no right or wrong way to make your house a home and put people at the center. Give yourself permission to do what works best for you.

⋙ **Get rid of storage.** *What?* I know, I know. Isn't that a cardinal sin? Doesn't every Realtor brag about all the storage a house has? So why should you get rid of some?

Because you'll fill it. You and I hate to leave an empty shelf, an uncrowded closet rod, a spare drawer. We'll add more stuff. Before we know it, we've added clutter, lost time, and increased stress to our lives.

Our house had an excessive amount of storage space when we bought it. But we were serious about not wanting to go back to our old ways of accumulating stuff. So we got creative about using some

of that space for something more functional.

Example: Our master bedroom had three giant closets. I mean seriously. C'mon. Who needs that many clothes? So we got rid of two closets and kept one. One closet was adjacent to the bathroom, so we knocked out a wall and absorbed the closet's footprint into the bathroom, making it less cramped. We turned the other closet into a cozy coffee nook. It's one of my favorite spaces in our house.

If having too much storage is tempting you to accumulate more, get rid of temptation by thinking outside the box. What else could that space become? Don't need a three-car garage? Maybe that extra bay could become a den or an outdoor gathering space. Don't need a linen closet? Create a little reading cubby for a child. Don't need so many kitchen cabinets? Move your linens into a few of them. You get the idea. Get creative. Do what works best for your home and your family.

15

welcome home

How grateful I was for our dumpster-fire-turned-vineyard-retreat of a home as my pregnancy progressed. I took full advantage of its peaceful simplicity. I would curl up in front of the stone fireplace and savor the view through floor-to-ceiling windows we had left curtainless. The room had such a light, airy feel, partly because of an abundance of natural light and partly because I was careful not to cram it with furniture. In fact, rather than add more chairs, we hung two simple wooden swings from a crossbeam, which kept the room open and added a touch of whimsy.

One of my favorite rooms is our living room, which has a high ceiling with exposed beams. Those beams have a story of their own to tell: The previous owner had stained them a dark reddish brown, but my mom and I decided that the heavy brown color wouldn't do. It looked too Tudor or Bavarian. We wanted the beams to be a natural wood color to match the airy feel of that space, whose soaring windows filled the room with light.

With the help of ladders, scaffolding, orbital sanders, stain strippers, and plenty of Advil for our sore necks and arms, Mom and I spent count-less hours sanding away the old stain. It was painstakingly slow work.

Once the last bit of stain was removed, we climbed down from our ladders and admired our work.

"The color of these timbers is perfect," Mom said. "They don't need stain. All they need is a clear sealant to protect the wood."

She was right. We coated the wood with sealant and left them unstained so their natural beauty could shine through. Wow, did the wood grain of those exposed beams add drama to the room's vibe!

As much as I loved nestling on the sofa under those gorgeous beams in our liv-ing room, I began to feel a bit stir-crazy as 2020 wore on. When I had the chance to get dressed up and go on a fancy dinner date with my hubby and some dear friends, nothing—not even a fast-approaching due date—would stop me.

Which explains what happens next.

At about four o'clock on Friday, November 20, Dino and I were getting ready for a night out. We had dinner plans with Sophie and James, owners of the winery we'd visited many months before. Because I take this going-out business seriously, I had painted my nails, done my hair all fancy in braids, and even shaved my legs—no small effort when thirty-seven weeks pregnant! I deserved an Olympic medal. My legs were lucky to escape with only a few small cuts and an impressive 60 percent of hair removed. Victory!

As I was getting ready, Dino sat soaking in the bathtub. I was sitting on the floor next to him while my toenails were drying when suddenly, I felt a little something. A little something . . . wet.

Uh-oh. I thought. *I know this feeling.*

"Babe!" I said, turning toward Dino. "I think my water broke a little."

"Are you serious?" Dino asked, wide-eyed. "Are you sure?"

I honestly wasn't sure if my water was breaking or if I'd just peed a little—which any woman in her ninth month of pregnancy can understand. With my other pregnancies, when my water broke, there was no doubt what was happening. I knew. Everyone knew. It was a flood. This wasn't that. Even so . . .

"I'm pretty sure my water is starting to break, babe. But we are still going out to dinner! I'm all dressed up. We have a sitter. My nails are done, my hair is done, and my legs! Feel my legs!" I grabbed his hand from out of the bathtub and made him feel one half-smooth leg, just to prove my point. "We. Are. Going. Out. To. Dinner."

"Well, maybe, but check in with your midwife at least," he said.

I called my midwife. "There was just a small amount of fluid," I told her. "It's nothing."

"It's not exactly nothing, though," she said. "Still, you're only thirty-seven weeks. Let's keep an eye on it for tonight. Just be sure to call if it starts gushing or if contractions kick in. Otherwise, let's talk again tomorrow."

That was all the permission I needed.

"Date night's still on!" I told Dino as I hung up.

"Fine," he said. "But if you start progressing, party's over and we come home. Deal?"

"Deal," I said. Wise man. Don't cross a thirty-seven-week-pregnant lady who has been promised a fancy meal with husband and friends.

Dinner was a blast. Laughing and dining with Sophie and James—oh, and laughing at the ridiculousness that is me, with my fancy dress and purse full of spare maxi pads.

We got home around ten o'clock that night, and Dino went into go mode. We had scheduled a home birth, partly due to the limitations placed on a hospital birth during the pandemic, and partly because, with a history of three easy deliveries, we liked the idea of welcoming Foxi into our family at home.

"I'll get the new sheets on the bed while you get into your PJs," he announced, his eyes bright. "Oh, I should probably vacuum in here, too—and then start a fire in the fireplace."

He was basically just running around on adrenaline, in anticipation of it all.

Well, we eventually went to bed on our new sheets (with a crinkly plastic sheet underneath). I was on high alert. With every little gurgle or kick, I wondered, *Is this it? Is it happening?*

Mind you, this was my fourth child, and with each of the previous pregnancies, I definitely knew when I was in labor. I'd be like, *Oh, yeah. This is it.* In my nervousness, I had simply forgotten what that was like.

Nothing happened that night . . . or all day Saturday. We weren't there yet.

By Sunday morning my water had truly broken, so the clock was now ticking. Typically, once your water breaks, contractions and labor should start progressing within twenty-four hours to avoid the risk of infection or worse.

I so badly wanted to have a home birth, and I was willing to do whatever I could to get the ball rolling. Just the idea of having to change our plans was stopping me from truly relaxing.

Dino and I took a few walks up and down our long, steep driveway, and I took all the natural remedies my midwife prescribed. Nothing worked. Foxi was taking her sweet time.

As evening approached, I started to get panicky. "If I don't start contracting by morning, we'll need to go to the hospital," I told Dino as we climbed into bed. "Foxi's safety comes first. But I really hope I go into labor so we can have her at home."

As I poured out my anxiety to Dino, he wrapped me in his arms.

"Let's pray about it," he said. And we did. We asked God for clarity in our decisions and for a safe delivery. Afterward, I fell into a fitful sleep. At 4:00 a.m., a strong contraction awoke me. *Oh yeah! There's that feeling I remember!*

I jumped out of bed. "Dino! It's happening!" I said, prodding him awake. A true contraction at last—and the end of the waiting. What a relief!

I spent the first hours of early labor in our bedroom, and later that morning my midwife arrived. When active labor began, so did the pain. I let my body lead the process. I had a giant exercise ball to lean into with each contraction, and I felt comfort in that ball. Dino sat behind me and rubbed my back as I breathed through the pain. For the next few hours, I rotated between walking our bedroom, soaking in our bathtub, and hugging that giant ball.

Finally, it was time to push. My goodness, the pain of childbirth is like no other. *Did it hurt this bad with my other three deliveries?* I wanted off this crazy ride, but there was only one way off: by getting this baby out. Time to go into beast mode.

I pushed one final time, and Foxi made her grand entrance into the world. A feeling of relief and pure euphoria flooded over me. Dino caught our newborn as she emerged, and the midwife masterfully untangled the umbilical cord from around her neck. And then at 1:21 p.m., November 23, the very best gift was placed in my arms: a sweet six-pound, seven-ounce baby girl, with eyes wide open, a dimple on her chin, and not a cry or peep out of her mouth.

As I lay there exhausted and elated, my new daughter stared straight into my eyes, her intense gaze piercing my soul.

Dino rushed from the receiving end of the bed, right up to my face. Kissing me, crying, and making sure I was okay, he whispered, "You did so good, Mama. You did so good."

"We did it!" I said. Forehead to forehead, we shared tears of sheer joy.

What a journey—from the tentative talk of adding to our family, to so many

> *"Dino! It's happening!" I said, prodding him awake. A true contraction at last—and the end of the waiting.*

deeper conversations, to Quinn's nightly prayers, and even through the vasectomy reversal—every step led to this moment: my husband and me holding this tiny gift of a healthy daughter in our arms.

 The sheer force of my wife's strength, both physical and emotional, never ceases to amaze me. Watching her bring Foxi into the world was a powerful experience I'll never forget.

And in that moment, just like that, we became a family of six. Quinn got the baby sister of her prayers, and the boys welcomed a little Fox who quickly stole their hearts. She was all eyes, gazing from face to face as we gathered around her and stared, which we were prone to do. We were smitten from day one. I still can't believe she's ours.

What a crazy ride it has been. When I look back over all the years of our marriage, a few memories stand out as turning points: I recall Ash and me in the trailer, our family tucked tightly inside, and nothing to our name but that 180-square-foot squeaky home on wheels. One evening as we lay in our tiny bedroom, I ran across a passage of Scripture that had been really meaningful to Ash after her miscarriage. It's from the book of James: "Consider it pure joy, my brothers and sisters, whenever you face trials of many kinds, because you know that the testing of your faith produces perseverance. Let perseverance finish its work so that you may be mature and complete, not lacking anything."[11]

Mature and complete? Yes, please. But being joyful and persistent through trials? Is that the required path?

I remember all too well the pain of losing a baby to miscarriage. Was that a trial I cared to repeat? Nope. I thought of those years of learning to surrender to God's plan rather than my own, of choosing to sacrifice for my family over my own desires. Did I want more of that slow, grinding growth, with its ups and downs and missteps along the way? Not really. *Be careful what you pray for, Dino.*

Then I thought of the flip side of those parts of our story and the trials Ash and I had faced thus far. Each trial, each season had in fact brought joy. Each carried gifts tucked beneath the pain. And through them, we had grown closer, been stretched as individuals, and slowly, slowly been transformed. We aren't the same people we were when we first got married.

Late one night after Ash finished nursing Foxi, she handed our baby to me. To help settle her down before returning her to the nursery, I began walking her around our living room. She stirred in her blanket, and two tiny hands stretched out toward me. I took one hand in my own and looked at her perfectly formed fingers and tiny nails. My heart just swelled with joy.

Part of that Scripture passage—"Consider it pure joy"—came to mind. Maybe the apostle James had been on to something. With those words echoing in my mind, I prayed silently:

Okay, Father, I am so filled with gratitude and happiness right now, I might burst. But I know life will bring more trials in the years to come. It's inevitable. And I know I could probably avoid some of them by choosing an easier life, one that just buys into our culture's message of "do what's best for you." But where will that get me? I want "mature and complete," and if that means taking the harder path—one that requires making sacrifices and considering our trials pure joy—then yes. I choose that path. I want growth and maturity over comfort. Ash and I have never loved comfort anyway. It's overrated. It's just not how we roll.

Father, help us guide our family along a path that doesn't shy away from doing hard things but faces them full on as we follow You.

It was scary praying that prayer. I mean, who prays for a harder life? For us, the easier path would not have led us to get rid of most of our possessions and move into a tiny trailer; or to buy a dumpster fire of a house during a pandemic and turn it into a home; or to add another child to our family at this point in our lives. But each of those choices, prayerfully made, held hidden lessons. If we had taken the easy path, we would have forfeited that knowledge.

Sitting here on the other side of a few trials, some large and some small, I can honestly say that this worldview of "do what feels best to you" is a myth. It's crap. It's a complete lie. By giving up your own desires to serve those you love or to follow God, you don't lose everything. In fact, you gain so much

> *I want growth and maturity over comfort. Ash and I have never loved comfort anyway. It's overrated.*

more. Ash and I both gave our lives over to Christ years ago, choosing to pursue God's path and seeking to make His way become ours. We have much to learn and much more growing to do, as our family and friends could tell you! But we're on the path. We're saying yes to "mature and complete." Our lives are truly so much more satisfying and complete when we're serving our family and following God. We wouldn't trade it for the world.

creating a child-friendly (not child-centric) home

A new baby, whether it's your first or your fourth, changes things. But it doesn't need to change everything. We kept things simple with Fox. Fourth time around, you realize you don't need every baby gadget on the market.

More stuff just causes more stress. This basic belief guides the principles that follow, which I hope you'll find helpful in creating a home your child will remember.

Design Your Child's Room

A child's room doesn't need to look like a playroom. It can be functional while still capturing the personality of its occupant. Whether you have a little space or a lot, you can make your child's room come to life. You just have to get creative.

By being intentional about furnishing a nursery with things your baby needs and you love, you will create a peaceful place for your little one. We converted a small study into a nursery rather than having Foxi share a room with Quinn. I wanted her nursery to be beautiful but functional since it would also serve as a guest room for company. We added a daybed, which functions as both a sofa and a single bed, against a window wall. I know one family who put a twin-full bunk bed (instead of twin-twin bunks) in their kids' shared room so that guests or sleepover buddies would have a bed of their own.

Nursery furniture can be super expensive. Instead, repurpose used furniture. I found some quality pieces at garage sales and on Craigslist, including an amazing antique chest of drawers that I refinished to use as Foxi's dresser.

Her room has no closet, so I got creative with some iron pipe and fittings from a hardware store. We installed a pole on one wall to hang her clothes, which looks cute and fits the farmhouse vibe of her room.

CREATING A CHILD-FRIENDLY (NOT CHILD-CENTRIC) HOME

⋙ **Less is more.** Not long after our firstborn, Gabe, arrived, I realized that I'd overcomplicated my life with a bunch of extra baby stuff. I remember being so excited when I got a baby-wipe warmer at a baby shower—something I'd registered for—but once Gabe was here, I found it just added extra clutter and a dangling electrical cord to the changing table. When you're a first-time mama, it's hard to know which gadgets are helpful and which just take up space. Reading blogs and asking friends about what to buy can be overwhelming, since everyone's style and opinions are different.

After Quinn was born, I'd given away all my baby stuff, so I was starting from scratch again with Foxi. This time, I kept it simple. I'd learned my lesson the first time around. Truth is, you don't need much. The basic necessities—diapers, wipes, car seat, diaper bag, some bottles for stored breast milk or formula, three or four comfy newborn outfits, and a few swaddling blankets make the list as newborn essentials, in my opinion. A few extras—maybe a baby monitor and a baby swing—and you're good to go. If you overdo it, you'll be robbed of simplicity.

With Fox, I started with less, and after she was born, if I felt like something was missing, I bought it. You can always pick up that must-have gadget later, once you know whether you really need it.

⋙ **Organize what you have.** It feels so good to open a drawer and see everything clearly organized inside, but baby clothes are so small that it's hard to keep them tidy. I love using bins inside of drawers so everything stays in place. No scouting around for the bottom half of that perfect baby outfit or matching socks.

I arranged Foxi's drawers like this: Top drawer for 0–3 months clothes and things I needed to grab quickly, like spare pacifiers or burp cloths. Second drawer for 3–6 months clothes, and the bottom drawer held her blankies and extra diapers.

Within each drawer, I use super cute bins I found at Target to keep small stuff from getting lost and diapers from flopping all over the place. They work great at helping Fox's onesies and socks stay organized. I also place a bin on top of the changing table to keep a few diapers and the wipes handy without making the area look cluttered.

>>> **Keep kid stuff in the kids' rooms.** In today's culture, we often feel pressure to make our lives child-centric, and one way that shows up is in the way toys and kid gear fill every room. It can seem like a good idea to keep lots of toys in the living area where your children play. The problem is, soon your whole house feels like their room.

When baby is little, it's fine to keep a small toy bin or basket in your family room. Once your child gets older, however, your home will feel more peaceful (and your kids will become more responsible for their belongings) when their stuff has its home inside their room.

Keeping toys in their own space brings more intentionality to play-time as well. One toy at a time is way less stressful for kids. A giant play-room filled with too many toys creates chaos and overstimulation—for the child and for you.

From an early age, we tried to teach our kids to play with one toy at a time and then put it away before getting out another one. Each toy is appreciated, and the children develop good habits about caring for their belongings. You will have created a home that is child-friendly, not child-centric.

>>> **New baby, same us.** Mama and Daddy may be sleepy from caring 24/7 for that cute little bundle, but it's still so important to make connecting with each other a top priority. It's what has kept Dino and me so close.

What does that connection time look like for you? Whether it's checking in on your significant other during the workday or setting aside time to connect each evening, find a way to make it happen. For us, that means a standing date night every evening after the kids go to bed. It's rarely anything fancy. We often just head to bed ourselves, snuggle together and talk, or watch a favorite sitcom or movie together. But it's a great way for us to reconnect at the end of the day. Giving the kids a set bedtime has made this possible. No matter how crazy a day with kids gets, Dino and I still focus on each other and our marriage every night.

>>> **Create a dependable rhythm.** Every family has its own routines for eating and sleeping. Your baby comes with no schedule. How will you help her adjust to the rhythm of life in your family?

While it's important for baby's attachment that we err on the side of meeting their needs quickly and reliably, we've found that following some sort of rhythm or schedule helps keep our home life more peaceful for everyone, baby included. It makes me a better mama if I know I'll likely have some downtime during the day, and it seems to give the baby added security in knowing, *First I eat, then I play, bathe, sleep*, etc. Finding and fostering a rhythm that fits your style is important because every family is different.

Flexibility is key. Go with what works best for you.

New babies are tiny, but what they lack in size, they make up for in the amount of change they usher into the family. As you and your family adjust, you won't always get it right. Your story and mine will forever be filled with bumps and beauty, missteps and miracles, which is what makes our stories worth telling. Let's make intentional choices in our homes—and our lives.

a closing note
from ashley

Two roads diverged in a wood, and I—
I took the one less traveled by,
And that has made all the difference.

—ROBERT FROST, "The Road Not Taken"

Open hands and an unclenched grip. That has been the Petrone posture since our trailer days, when we spent weeks and then months watching workers move dirt around on the scenic spot where we'd once pictured building our dream house. In that hard season, we learned the value of paying attention to God's stirring in our hearts and waiting for His clear direction on the next step for our lives.

Both Dino and I spend a lot of time—individually and together—listening for God's quiet voice in Scripture and in prayer. By being attentive to His leading in the small things, we've become more comfortable paying attention to the gentle nudges in our spirit that lead us to ask, *What do You have next for us?* And as we begin exploring what His answer might be, we've also learned to pray, *We don't want this unless it's from You.* We recognize the danger of presuming and running ahead of God's direction. Sometimes He is asking us to be content where we are and wait for Him to reveal His next step for us.

So when we'd finished most of the renovations on our home in Northern California, I wasn't surprised when I began to feel that familiar prodding in my spirit. Over the next several months and through a variety of circumstances, God directed our family again—this time all the way to Anna Maria Island off Florida's Gulf Coast to the four-unit property we bought there. We lived in a rental while we renovated it. Once the renovations were complete, we prepared to rent out the four units and buy a house nearby. The kids finished their school year from home and began attending the local Florida schools in the fall.

We named our new property Joie Inn. We couldn't think of a better name to reflect our family's passion for finding joy in the in-between, which is exactly

where we are as I write this—in the middle of making our inn a place of rest and renewal for our guests, and a place of sandy, sunny, saltwater adventures for our family.

We haven't cut our ties to California (most of our family still lives there after all), but we sold our vineyard home in the redwoods so that another family can experience the serenity of that place—and enjoy the quirky swings in the middle of our living room.

Once again, we hold our newest home with open hands, always alert for any prompting that may be God's way of leading us to our next adventure. In the meantime, we delight in our new home, whether watching Gabe spend joy-filled hours in the water or working alongside Dino's sister and her husband, who recently moved here from overseas. Home, I've learned, isn't so much a place as it is anywhere our family is gathered, delighting in God and one another.

As Dino and I look to the future, this is what we want for our family: to follow God and to say yes to His promptings, even if they're hard or unconventional. We don't ever want to sit in the comfortable. We don't want to doddle along an easy, complacent path. We want to crush each challenge, face our trials full on, and savor every experience that comes our way. We want to lay our heads on our pillows at night knowing we're a little stronger, a little less selfish, and maybe a little more like Jesus than we were the day before.

I'm a designer at heart. One of the things I love most about design is that it's such a great word picture for transformation in our lives. Just as it takes intention-ality to transform a room or a house, it takes intentionality to transform our lives. It means getting rid of things we don't need, love, or have room for. It means adding only those things that we adore, treasures that are perfect for our particular life.

Will you join us? Let's take the path we sense God leading us toward, even if it's uncomfortable or unconventional. Let's release our grip on what we thought a perfect life should look like and invite God to guide us into a life that more fully honors Him. By unclenching our grip and choosing to follow His lead, we discover a life that is far more fulfilling, rewarding, and transforming.

My prayer for you is this: that you may design your life with intention, face your trials head-on with God at your side, and find joy in the in-between.

Just as it takes intentionality
to transform a room or a house,
it takes intentionality to transform our lives.

a letter from
dino to his kids

Gabe, Gavin, Quinn, and Foxi,

One day you'll be old enough to appreciate that this book is a love letter between your mother and me. It's also a love letter to you.

I've loved you kids from the moment you were born, and yet with each of you, there was a specific moment when I remember falling head over heels in love. It was different every time.

Gabe, it was when you and I were lying on the floor of your room, playing. You were around ten months and had just learned to crawl over the top of me. You were so proud! My love for you hit me like a ton of bricks. I was proud too.

Gavin, it was when you were just a few months old and you got a really high temperature. We rushed you to the hospital and I remember looking at your flushed face in a panic. I could not imagine living a minute of this life without you in it.

Quinn, it was the moment you turned your huge eyes to me in the hospital on the day you were born. You read about that moment in these pages, love.

And little Fox, our love story began when you were just an idea and I first saw your name on a TV screen. In that moment, I felt like God gave me just a glimpse of what life could look like with you in it. I could see us together laughing, crying, or just walking hand in hand.

Kids, if you're reading this, it means you're old enough to begin recognizing that while you're my children, you are also individuals. You're old enough to live your life the way you see fit. And you're old enough to notice how I live my life—a scary thought for every parent. You know my shortcomings. And hopefully, too, you know that to the best of my ability, I try to live my life to honor Jesus Christ. I've found it to be the most rewarding path I could ever imagine, and it's the path I hope you, too, will choose.

The things you so fervently search for, the things deep in your heart and soul, the human ache that longs to be filled—God is the only one who can fill that void and deliver what your hearts long for. Seek after Him with your whole heart, and He will give you back everything in return.

I love you.

Dad

how to date your spouse

One of the unexpected surprises for me in reading comments from my @arrowsandbow community on Instagram has been seeing the interest readers express in my marriage to Dino. Evidently, like me, many people want to get better at growing their most important relationships.

It's easy to get lost in the daily grind of work, kids, life—basically putting everything before our marriages. As we close these pages, I thought I'd share a few of the things Dino and I do to take our marriage to the next level of intimacy and connection.

The Year of the Bathy. For more than a year, our country (and the world) was pretty shut down due to the COVID-19 pandemic. Restaurants, movie theaters, and anything deemed nonessential was closed, so there were few places to go for fun. That was a bummer for the date-night scene, so Dino and I got creative.

We labeled 2020 the Year of the Bathy. We did our best to set aside a few nights a week to take a bath together. We'd let the kids watch a movie or play games in the other room while we shared this private time together. It wasn't just sexy; it was relationally intimate. Being stripped down and vulnerable allowed for some really personal and deep conversations.

Give it a try. Pour some soothing tea or a glass of wine for each of you and enjoy them over conversation in the tub. If your house doesn't have a bathtub, try sitting together in the shower with the water gently spraying over you, or even snuggling together in bathrobes on your bed. Simply hanging out naked (or nearly naked) and talking will slow your life down enough to help you really connect.

Date nights. When Dino and I don't prioritize alone time with one another, it's easy to drift from being on the same page about our family, our relationship, and life in general—and dating each other is a great way to stay connected. If we go too long without a date night, we find there's less communication and more friction in our marriage.

Date nights cost money, but if you're able to set aside a few dollars every week, you can invest those dollars on an evening out. Hire a sitter (if you have kids) and spend your dollars on dinner, a movie, a round of mini golf, or whatever you both enjoy. The goal is to do something that brings you together and adds fun to your relationship.

At-home date nights. If going out isn't an option, at-home date nights can be just as fruitful. If your kids are too young to fend for themselves, start your date night after their bedtime. If they're older, feed them early, throw on a movie, and let them know, "Unless someone is bleeding, don't knock on Mommy and Daddy's door." I'm kidding—but only a little. Just be sure to carve out alone time consistently.

Gamifying your relationship. Playing together with your spouse or significant other is a great way to build closeness. He or she is your best friend, after all. If you both enjoy doing puzzles or playing cards and board games, then build those activities into your weekends.

Start a challenge with your spouse to keep things interesting and spicy. I know a couple who plays games together for "chore points." Whoever wins, the other person will do a chore for them—load the dishwasher, fold a load of laundry, or pick up the kids from soccer practice. Dino and I sometimes play card games or board games to earn massages from each other. We'll even let the kids make up a challenge for us. It's a fun way to get them involved in Mommy and Daddy's connection and sets a sweet example for them.

We love doing the Pancake Challenge or Upward Spiral game (as described in chapter 11), and we'll sometimes change it up to make it more interesting by adding in elements that fit our personal needs and desires.

Get creative and have fun with each other. Your relationship is worth the investment.

discussion guide

1. In addition to their physical attraction, what drew Dino and Ashley together so quickly? Describe a time you connected quickly with someone who became a good friend, trusted coworker, or spouse.

2. Ashley describes how she made their first apartment into a cozy home—despite its small size and a small budget. What makes a space feel like home to you?

3. Describe the core issues behind the problems Dino and Ashley experienced in the first year of their marriage. Can you relate to any of them? If so, in what way?

4. Dino explains how he found gaming to be a fun way to engage the part of his brain that likes to solve problems. Ashley gravitated toward shopping for home decor and using her design sense. Name an interest or hobby you pursue that reflects your way of thinking or one of your talents.

5. Ashley's miscarriage was the first major loss she and Dino had ever experienced. How did they respond to this difficulty? How have you responded to your own heartaches? Can you think of a time when you experienced "authentic connection and comfort in times of sorrow" (see page 50)? If so, explain.

6. Have you ever had a "hobby jobby"—a way to make money by pursuing a hobby or favorite pastime? If so, explain. If not, do you have a hobby you'd like to turn into a "jobby"? How might you get started?

7. The Petrones' marriage began to change when Dino made a decision to prioritize his family and Ashley determined to cherish Dino rather than criticize him. What is the best relationship advice you've ever received? If you took it to heart, what happened?

8. Why do you think Arrows and Bow (@arrowsandbow) took off on Instagram? How does its success reflect some of the benefits of connecting over social media?

9. What did you think of Dino and Ashley's decision to sell their five-bedroom Moorpark home and move into a 180-square-foot trailer? Have you ever made a drastic life decision that surprised your friends or family? If so, explain. Are you glad you made that decision? What would you do differently?

10. What did you learn from the ways the Petrone family adapted to their limited space, skeptical friends, and construction delays? How might you apply one of those lessons when addressing a current dilemma in your own life?

11. How did Ashley and Dino respond when it became clear that the home they'd dreamed of building would never be built? Have you ever had to give up on a dream? How did that affect you?

12. Dino and Ashley say that the seventeen months their family lived in the trailer was the best thing that could have happened to them. Based on how they approached life post-trailer, how would you say that experience changed them? Have you ever lived through a difficult season that brought unexpected blessings? If so, explain.

13. A couple of chance conversations got Dino and Ashley thinking about having a fourth baby. Has a random interaction with someone ever led you to make an unexpected decision? Explain.

14. Have you ever made a large purchase—like a home, a vehicle, or a computer—that turned out to be a Hot-Mess Express? What did that experience teach you—whether about renovation or repair, yourself, or other people?

15. "Open hands and an unclenched grip" is how Ashley describes the Petrone approach to life (see page 275). How would you sum up your current approach? If you don't want to continue living that way, what changes do you need to make? How could consciously adopting a positive life motto improve the way you live?

notes

1. "How Much Sleep Do Children Need?" WebMD, accessed June 16, 2021, https://www.webmd.com/parenting/guide/sleep-children#1.

2. Ashley Petrone, "Me Doing Me," *Arrows and Bow* (blog), July 9, 2016, https://www.arrowsandbow.com/me-doing-me.

3. 1 Corinthians 13:11.

4. The book was *Cherish: The One Word that Changes Everything for Your Marriage* by Gary Thomas (Grand Rapids, MI: Zondervan, 2017).

5. Matthew 5:37, ESV.

6. Acts 20:35.

7. Lysa TerKeurst, *Uninvited: Living Loved When You Feel Less Than, Left Out, and Lonely* (Nashville: Thomas Nelson, 2016).

8. A granny flat (also called an ADU—adult dwelling unit) is a self-contained, one- or two-bedroom home located on the grounds of a single-family home.

9. Dino and I often unwind by watching reruns of *The Office*. In season 4, episode 9, "The Dinner Party," Michael Scott describes the toll of undergoing a vasectomy and then having it reversed—or as he calls it, "Snip-snap, snip-snap, snip-snap!"

10. Luke 12:48, NIV.

11. James 1:2-4, NIV.

about the authors

Ashley and Dino Petrone have been married since 2006 and make their home in Florida with their four kids: Gabe, Gavin, Quinn, and Foxi. Ashley began her popular Instagram account @arrowsandbow as a way to document her home-design journey. It took off during the seventeen months their family lived in the 180-square-foot trailer she'd transformed from an outdated RV into a bright and welcoming home. Dino is a senior engineer, and Ashley is a full-time mom, blogger, and interior designer.

Visit them online at arrowsandbow.com.